Reynolds Wrap
Creative Cooking
with aluminum foil

by Eleanor Lynch
Director of Home Economics
Reynolds Metals Company

A BENJAMIN COMPANY / RUTLEDGE BOOK
Distributed by
Grosset & Dunlap, Inc.

Published by The Benjamin Company, Inc.
485 Madison Avenue, New York, New York 10022
Distributed by Grosset & Dunlap, Inc.
Third Printing 1968

Introduction

Practically everybody today is interested in food—not just any kind of food but the very best. And not just those dishes mother used to make but the fine foods of other countries and of every region of this country.

The beauty, convenience and abundance offered by our food markets all make food preparation easy and introduce us to many foods far outside our own family experience. This has stimulated a great new interest in cooking—spurred on by beautiful pictures and articles in magazines and newspapers, by TV commercials, by the programs given by great food experts, and by their cookbooks.

One of our top news magazines recently made a survey of both full-time homemakers and women who combine business with homemaking. They found that women enjoy and use convenience foods extensively. But they also found that when they want to serve guests or put special effort into a meal, they still take down a recipe book and cook from scratch. Apparently cooking is one area where almost anyone with the guidance of a good cookbook can feel creative, artistic and imaginative.

Not to be forgotten are the men who like to cook. Male celebrities are often featured, proclaiming their culinary skills. Almost every man has a few favorite recipes he delights in preparing for his family and friends. And, of course, the outdoor cooking field is truly a man's world.

This cookbook is designed to tell you how Reynolds Wrap® aluminum foil can be used to make food preparation easier, to help you cook with less fuss and fewer dishes and to do away with most of the clean-up that frequently spoils the fun you've had cooking a fine meal. In addition, we present some of our favorite recipes to prepare with a gourmet flair—the kind you like to serve to an especially appreciative group.

This book will teach you secrets of using Reynolds Wrap to make your cooking more pleasurable and the results more delectable.

—Eleanor Lynch

PHOTO CREDITS

Bill Helms—pages 28-29; 76-77. Laszlo—cover; pages 1; 4-5; 12-13; 68-69; 92-93; 100-101; 108-109; 124-125; 180-181. Joe Singer—pages 52-53; 116-117; 140-141; 164-165.

Contents

The Uses of Aluminum Foil

What is aluminum foil—that magic material now a household staple? It's pure aluminum; a large block of the solid metal is rolled, much as pie crust is rolled, until it becomes a long, thin, continuous sheet.

Aluminum is friendly to food—it's one of the elements most commonly found in the earth and is present in all foods. That is why it is the ideal wrap for use with food.

When to use regular 12-inch-wide aluminum foil: Use this lighter weight foil for wrapping foods to be stored in the refrigerator, for sandwich wrapping, packaging cookies to send through the mail, for short-term freezing and many other uses.

When to use heavy duty 14-inch broiling or 18-inch all-purpose foil: This is the foil for lining the broiler pan and the outdoor grill. Use it, too, for lining roasting and baking pans, for roasting the turkey and wrapping foods to be baked in the oven and for all uses where liquids are to be held secure with no leakage.

Heavy duty is the foil for freezing, too, since it provides the best protection against drying out, loss of flavor and color.

Let's clear up the old question, which side should go on the outside, the shiny or the dull? It really does not matter. In rolling, one side of the foil becomes shiny; the other—not in contact with the heavy roller—comes out with a mat finish.

Here are other tips on foil use:

Don't use too much foil—just enough to conform to the pan or just enough to wrap or seal the food. More than enough serves no purpose and may delay heat penetration.

Tight sealing—it's not always necessary. Even when foil is just loosely folded over food, flavors and much moisture are held in. Airtight sealing is directed in some recipes where all liquid must be prevented from evaporating.

Puncturing—it is a fact that sharp bones, the use of sharp kitchen tools or too rough handling will puncture foil. Heavy duty is stronger than standard, but all foils must be used with a little care to avoid puncturing.

Will foil catch fire in the oven or broiler? No indeed. It is not flammable. But if a sheet of foil is placed on the rack of a broiler pan, with fatty steaks or chops directly on the foil, and the pan then placed under the broiler, the melting fat on the foil may get so hot it catches fire. Similarly, lining an ordinary pie pan or other shallow pan with foil and attempting to broil fatty meat on the foil is bad practice.

Be sure to follow instructions, page 32, for proper broiling. *Can I line my oven with foil?* Yes, if you line it properly. In electric ranges, the rod which carries the current is just above the bottom of the oven. This may be lifted up and a sheet of foil placed underneath. Smooth this foil so it fits flat on the oven bottom. In gas ranges, the burner which heats the oven is under the bottom of the oven and heat enters through openings either in the oven bottom or along the sides. Be sure to cut out openings to conform to those in the oven bottom before placing foil in position.

Foil used on the bottom of the oven reflects heat upwards and protects the floor from drips and crumbs.

Don't try to cover a shelf in the oven with foil, as this will interfere with heat circulation. If you wish to use foil to catch boilovers from a pie or casserole dish, use a small piece just a little larger than the food and don't place it on the same shelf. Place it on a lower shelf so some heat circulates under the food. Turn up the edges of the foil all around to catch the liquid.

Discoloration or pitting of foil. Some foods will cause a slight discoloration on foil—it is similar to the tarnishing of silver, and is harmless. Some foods high in salt or acid or both may cause perforations in foil. Cold cuts, spaghetti sauce and salad mixtures are offenders.

Why does poultry skin sometimes stick to foil? The skin of chicken and turkey has a gelatinous substance which sometimes sticks to foil or anything it comes in contact with. When roasting poultry in foil, prevent this from happening by placing a few slices of onion, carrot and/or celery on the foil, then placing the bird on the vegetables. This prevents direct contact with the foil. When wrapping poultry be sure it is brushed with soft butter, margarine or other fat. Wrap loosely and don't seal airtight.

To Begin With

To Begin With

Spur-of-the-moment or state occasion—any meal can start off with tasty appetizers—and foil will help you prepare them

Every homemaker wants to have on hand a supply of tidbits and snacks to serve drop-in guests. From time to time there's the exciting problem of giving a big party—and, more frequently, the elegant buffet or seated dinner to observe a holiday or other occasion, which requires a very special beginning.

Appetizers, canapes and hors d'oeuvres for all these occasions are a much-enjoyed part of the entertaining scene. They can make your reputation as a hostess. With the help of Reynolds Wrap, you can serve savory tidbits at a moment's notice.

A good and easy appetizer—make in advance, take from the freezer, bake quickly and serve hot.

CHEESE DOLLARS *(4 dozen)*

½ pound natural mild Cheddar, in small pieces	*1 cup sifted flour*
	⅛ teaspoon salt
	Generous grating of pepper
½ cup butter	

Let cheese stand at room temperature until soft. Cream butter; add cheese and whip with electric mixer until well blended. Add flour sifted with salt and pepper. Mix thoroughly. Chill until firm, then form into 3 rolls about 1 inch in diameter. Wrap each roll in foil and chill or freeze. To serve: Thaw frozen rolls briefly, cut in ¼-inch slices, and arrange ½ inch apart on foil-covered cookie sheet. Bake in 425°F oven 8 to 10 minutes, until *very* lightly browned. Serve hot or cold on a pretty tray or plate.

HURRY-UP APPETIZERS

Guests coming and you're not prepared? Make up these appetizers 30 minutes ahead—if there's time. Arrange them on a foil-covered cookie sheet, cover with foil and refrigerate.

In color picture: Stuffed Mushrooms, Seafood Puffs, Chutney Cheese Canapes, Allumettes, Bacon-Wrapped Snickles, Vegetable Appetizers

When the doorbell rings, remove foil cover and brown the appetizers briefly under the broiler. Slip foil with the hot appetizers onto a pretty tray and garnish with cherry tomatoes and parsley. Crimp foil to make a pretty border.

CHUTNEY CHEESE CANAPES

Spread toast rounds or crackers with English chutney, then sprinkle liberally with grated sharp Cheddar cheese.

"SISKIJON OYSTERS"

Place thin slices of dill pickle on toast rounds. Top with cubes of Cheddar cheese.

SEAFOOD PUFFS

Remove any shell or membrane from ½ pound cooked shrimp or crabmeat and chop fine. Combine with 1 cup mayonnaise, 1 tablespoon lemon juice, ½ teaspoon salt and a few drops of Tabasco. Place spoonfuls on toast rounds or crackers. Top each with a small piece of shrimp, dipped in mayonnaise. This is enough for forty 1½-inch rounds of bread.

To make toast rounds: Cut thin slices of white or dark bread in 1½-inch rounds. Arrange on foil-covered cookie sheet. Place under broiler and brown lightly, turning with pancake turner to brown second side. Cool. Store in a foil package at room temperature. They'll keep for 3 weeks.

ROLL-UPS

Remove crusts from thin slices of white bread. Spread with deviled ham or other savory, finely chopped meat, cheese, or seafood mixture. Roll up jelly roll fashion, fasten with toothpicks if necessary. Arrange on foil, brush with melted butter, and refrigerate.

BACON-WRAPPED SNICKLES

Partially cook bacon so most of the fat is removed. Then cut bacon strips in half or in suitable length and wrap around any of the foods listed below. Secure with a toothpick. Arrange on foil-covered cookie sheet and refrigerate until guests arrive. Place under the broiler until bacon is crisp and the food hot or cooked.

Slide the foil with these tidbits onto a serving tray or keep them hot on an electric warming tray or in the electric casserole.

Here are foods to wrap and broil: Pineapple cubes ... Stuffed olives ... Prunes stuffed with walnuts or candied pineapple ... Raw oysters ... Raw shrimp ... Raw scallops ... Chicken livers (cut them in half) ... Pickled watermelon rind (drained).

FRUIT APPETIZERS

Suitable fruits are apples, pears, canteloupes, bananas and pine-apple and firm, not too juicy, orange sections. Cut fruit into wedges or spears leaving skin on. Dip in lemon juice; arrange on serving dish, cover with foil, and chill in refrigerator until needed. They will stay fresh without discoloring about 6 hours. Place a bowl of curry- or Roquefort-flavored dip in center. Garnish with firm grapes, whole strawberries with hulls on, bing cherries . . . any colorful fruit in season.

BROILED MUSHROOMS

Select medium-size fresh mushrooms, or use drained canned mushroom caps. Chop stems with a small amount of onion. Sauté in butter, adding salt and pepper to taste. Sauté chicken livers, chop and season well, adding the sautéed stems, or use liverwurst or chopped cooked ham. Fill caps. Cover with foil and refrigerate. Before serving, remove cover, brown under broiler 6 to 8 minutes.

VEGETABLE APPETIZERS

Prepare these vegetables ahead, wrap in foil and refrigerate. Serve beautifully cold and crisp with one of the tasty dips that follow.

Carrots—Scrape and cut lengthwise in strips, then crosswise in 3- to 4-inch lengths.

Cauliflower—Separate flowers and trim the stalks a bit to make them easy to handle when dunking.

Celery—Trim tender stalks; cut lengthwise in ½-inch strips, then crosswise in finger lengths.

Radishes—Remove root ends and trim off all leaves except a few center ones; make several cuts from root end toward stem end and drop into ice-cold water to make radish roses.

Belgian Endive—Cut in lengthwise strips or separate into leaves.

Cucumbers—Peel, cut in half lengthwise and remove center if seeds are large; then cut in strips and, if cucumbers are long, cut strips crosswise.

Zucchini—Use small ones, cut in half lengthwise, then in strips.

Cherry Tomatoes—Wash, leave blossom end on.

Fennel—Remove outside tough stalks. Trim feathery tops, leaving just the tenderest greenest portion. Cut the whole bulb-like end right up through the stalks.

Make these dips ahead. Cover bowl with foil, chill in refrigerator before using. Scooped-out small cabbage, green pepper—even a handsome turnip—make a nice dip holder.

CHILI DIP   *(1½ cups)*

    ¼ cup chili sauce   *¼ teaspoon salt*
    1 tablespoon lemon juice   *Dash pepper*
    2 tablespoons tomato   *¾ cup mayonnaise*
      ketchup   *½ cup dairy sour cream*
    3 drops Tabasco

Add chili sauce, lemon juice, ketchup, Tabasco, salt and pepper to mayonnaise; mix well and add sour cream.

CURRY DIP   *(2½ cups)*

    8 ounces cream cheese   *1 teaspoon lemon juice*
    ½ cup dairy sour cream   *¼ teaspoon salt*
    1½ tablespoons curry   *1 cup chutney, finely*
      powder   *chopped*

Cream together cheese and sour cream. Add remaining ingredients and mix well.

SPECIAL OCCASION HORS D'OEUVRES

Here are recipes for the gourmet cook who doesn't mind spending time and effort in creating something different and truly delicious. They are haute cuisine—served by the most elegant restaurants—but you'll find that you can make them at home with little trouble, and they'll taste as good or better. Reynolds Wrap helps in the preparation of these delights, all of which may be passed on prettily garnished serving dishes at a cocktail party, or served as the first course at a buffet.

BATONNETS DE FROMAGE   *(5 dozen)*

    5 tablespoons butter   *2 egg yolks, beaten*
    5 tablespoons flour   *Flour*
    1½ cups milk   *1 egg*
    ¾ teaspoon salt   *¼ cup milk*
    ¾ cup grated imported   *Bread crumbs*
      Parmesan cheese

Melt butter in a large saucepan, add flour; cook, stirring until mixture has bubbled for 3 to 4 minutes. Add milk and salt. Cook, stirring constantly, until mixture thickens. Add cheese, stir until it melts. Add a little of the hot mixture to the egg yolks, mix well, return to the saucepan. Cook and stir very gently 2 to 3 minutes longer. Line a 5 x 9 x ¾ inch pan with foil; pour in the mixture. Cool and cover with foil. Chill overnight.

When firm, turn mixture out on floured board; peel off the foil, and cut mixture in little rectangles ½ x 1½ inches. Roll in flour; dip in a mixture of 1 egg beaten with ¼ cup of milk; roll in fine dry bread crumbs. Place on sheets of Reynolds Wrap on a cookie sheet. Freeze. When firm, package the little batonnets in foil pans, 24 or more to the pan, overwrapping in foil. Store in freezer. They keep 6 weeks. Foil pans from purchased cakes are excellent for this.

To serve, let stand 5 minutes at room temperature; then fry a few at a time in deep hot fat. Serve hot, 2 or 3 to a person, on a small plate with a fork. Garnish with:
French Fried Parsley—this is nothing more than little sprigs of well-drained parsley, tossed into the fat and fried for 30 seconds. It's traditional with these creamy-centered little cheese croquettes.

Although this sounds grand and is served as an elegant appetizer with beverages, it is simply cream puff mixture to which Swiss cheese has been added. The dough may be baked in a long strip or in tiny balls the size of cherries. It may be made a week or more ahead and frozen.

GOUGÈRE *(24 servings)*

1 cup boiling water	*½ teaspoon salt*
½ cup butter or	*4 eggs, unbeaten*
margarine	*1 cup coarsely grated*
1 cup sifted all-purpose	*Swiss cheese*
flour	

Bring the boiling water and butter to a boil in a medium-size saucepan. When the butter is melted, add the flour and salt all at once. Reduce the heat and stir vigorously until the mixture leaves the sides of the pan and begins to gather into a ball. Remove from heat and add the eggs, one at a time, beating vigorously after each. Continue beating until the mixture has a satin sheen. Stir in the cheese. Place a sheet of heavy duty foil on a cookie sheet. Spread the mixture on the foil in 2 strips about 1½ inches wide, at least 4 inches apart. Pile up each strip as high as possible. Bake in 400°F oven 50 minutes, or until light golden brown and firm to the touch. Remove; prick sides of the strips in a few places with a sharp fork.

Turn off heat and return to oven for 5 minutes. To serve immediately, arrange on attractive tray or plate, cut in 1-inch slices. Serve hot or warm.

Tiny puffs: Drop Gougère mixture from a teaspoon onto foil-covered cookie sheet. Bake in 400°F oven 30 minutes.

To freeze: Cool strips or puffs. Place in freezer until firm. Wrap in heavy duty foil. To serve, remove from freezer, unwrap, thaw 10 minutes. Reheat and crisp in 350°F oven 10 minutes. Slice the long strips diagonally; serve puffs just as they are.

ALLUMETTES   *(36 servings)*

RICH PASTRY
2 cups sifted all-purpose
  flour
1 teaspoon salt
⅓ cup butter
⅓ cup shortening
5 tablespoons cold water

FILLING
1 tablespoon chopped
  onion
½ cup minced mushrooms
1½ cups finely chopped
  leftover chicken or
  ham
1 cup thick chicken
  gravy or white sauce
Seasonings

Sift flour and salt. Cut in buttter and shortening; sprinkle with water, mixing lightly with a fork. Divide pastry into two pats; wrap in Reynolds Wrap and chill for an hour or longer. Sauté onion and mushrooms in butter until just tender. Add meat, gravy to make a thick, very moist mixture, and seasonings. Cool. Roll each pastry pat into a rectangle about 9 x 6 inches. Arrange filling lengthwise down one long side of pastry, centering it, leaving ⅜-inch edges uncovered. Moisten these edges, then fold the unspread side over the filling, making a filled pastry 3 inches wide. Press edges firmly together on all four sides of filling. Wrap in heavy duty foil and freeze until needed.

To serve: Remove from freezer; remove foil and place each filled pastry on a cookie sheet. Cut through at ½-inch intervals, separate slightly, and bake at 425°F for 20 to 30 minutes, or until nicely browned. Separate as you remove them from the pan. Serve hot.

Good to know: Can be made with any savory leftover meat. Unbaked Allumettes keep 6 weeks in freezer.

Soups
to Serve,
to Save

Soups to Serve, to Save

Soup from the freezer, any old time—with more flavor, less fuss than ever before

Here are ways to have rich-flavored homemade soups without going through a lengthy preparation each time they are to be served. Make up such ever-useful soups as beef broth and chicken broth in quantity and freeze them. Make up just the thick base for soups such as split pea, chowders and cream soups and freeze these concentrates. Add extra liquid at time of serving.

This way, you can have your own homemade French onion soup, hearty and flavorful split pea, gourmet black bean and extra-special treats like Vichyssoise and Lobster Bisque—all in a matter of minutes.

SOUP FREEZING TIPS

Freezing leftovers: The end of a roast, a leftover chicken carcass, trimmings from meat and poultry, the ham bone, leftover vegetables—if you haven't time or inclination to use them, wrap them in foil, label, and freeze. They can all go into the soup pot on a soup-making day.

Freezing soup or soup base after it is made: Cool mixtures as quickly as possible so they'll keep all their flavor. (Set the pan in ice water for extra-quick cooling.) Select containers which will hold the amounts needed for the number of people you expect to serve. Pint- or quart-size bowls, pans or baking dishes you have on hand make excellent freezing containers.

If you use your regular bowls and dishes, you won't want to keep them tied up in the freezer. Here's the trick: Line them with Heavy Duty Reynolds Wrap. An easy way is to mold a piece of foil over the outside of the bowl or dish, then fit it inside. Pour cooled soup into the containers, allowing space for expansion at the top during freezing. Cover with foil; place in the freezer on a flat surface so they won't spill.

In color picture: Tomato Soup Base

When the soup is solidly frozen, remove the foil liner with its frozen block of soup. Seal the foil liner with the top covering or give the soup an overwrap of foil. Label, return to the freezer.

Serving the frozen soups: Take soup from freezer and remove foil. If foil sticks, quickly run cold water over it. Place soup in a saucepan and heat gently. If it is concentrated, begin diluting it with the liquid called for in the recipe. Add part of the liquid first and, as the soup thaws, continue adding liquid until desired consistency is reached.

Soups to be served cold are first heated in the same way and diluted to the right consistency. Heat only enough to blend, then beat with electric mixer or whirl in a blender and rechill. Add salt and pepper to all soups after thawing, since only a small amount is used in preparing them for freezing.

You may like to make up these recipes and serve part immediately, freeze the remainder. In any event, they are like money in the bank, just wonderful to have on hand.

Beef broth or "stock" is a basic soup with many uses, not a concentrated base. Fresh vegetables, barley, noodles or other pasta may be added when it is heated for serving. It is an ingredient in French Onion Soup, can be used for diluting black bean and other hearty soups. It adds richer flavor than water to sauces and gravies.

BEEF BROTH OR BROWN SOUP STOCK   *(16 servings)*

4 pounds beef bones	*3 stalks celery with tops*
2 pounds veal bones	*2 leeks (if available)*
1 large carrot, sliced	*1 onion*
1 large onion, sliced	*1 carrot*
5½ quarts water	*Few sprigs parsley*
2 teaspoons salt	*1 clove garlic*
2 pounds soup beef	*10 peppercorns*
1 2-pound can tomatoes	

Spread bones, sliced carrot, and onion in a large, shallow foil-lined pan; roast in 400°F oven for about 40 minutes or until well browned. Remove to a very large kettle. Add 5 quarts water, salt, soup beef. Bring slowly to a boil, skimming as foam rises to the surface. Put remaining ½ quart water in roasting pan and return to oven until all the browned juices are dissolved; add to the kettle. When foam ceases to rise, add remaining ingredients. Cover; cook very slowly without stirring for about 4 hours. Skim if necessary.

Ladle out meat, bones, and vegetables carefully, disturbing soup as little as possible. Save meat, discard bones and vegetables. Place cheesecloth, wrung out in cold water, in a large strainer over a large bowl. Ladle out soup carefully into strainer. Cool strained soup uncovered, then chill in refrigerator until fat hardens on surface. Remove fat. If broth has jelled, reheat until melted. Fill foil-lined bowls or pans and freeze. Makes 4 quarts.

Meat may be sliced and served as Boiled Beef with Horseradish Sauce. If you wish to use this simply as a hearty, flavorful beef-and-vegetable soup, after the fat has been removed and broth reheated, add diced vegetables such as carrots, celery, onion. Cook 5 to 10 minutes until they are tender. Add meat cut into small dice. Cool quickly; freeze. To serve, heat, add salt and pepper; garnish with chopped parsley.

SOUP FROM FROZEN LEFTOVERS

Follow the general proportions for Beef Broth. Leftovers can be of two types—cooked leftovers from roasts and uncooked leftovers consisting of trimmings, bones from roasts the butcher has boned for you, and other uncooked meats that you may have stored until there was time to use them.

Soup from cooked leftovers only will need special attention to flavoring ingredients . . . plenty of onion, celery, parsley, etc. If a combination of cooked and uncooked meats and bones can be used, the soup will have more flavor. Brown frozen uncooked bones without defrosting; do not bother to defrost any soup-making ingredients. Mild-flavored leftover frozen vegetables, cooked or uncooked, may be added to soup.

Your own full-flavored, tender chicken and chicken broth—make it up frequently and keep it on hand in your freezer, for you can do so much with it! It's wonderful for feeding the baby and youngsters with just the addition of rice or pastina. Serve it as old fashioned chicken soup, adding noodles and a few vegetables.

CHICKEN AND BROTH BASE   *(18 to 20 servings)*

3 broiler-fryers (2½ to 3 pounds)   *Handful of parsley sprigs*
6 quarts water   *10 peppercorns*
4 medium onions   *1 teaspoon salt*
6 stalks celery with leaves   *3 small bay leaves*

Rinse chicken and place in a large kettle with water, vegetables, and seasonings. Bring to a boil; skim off any foam that rises to the top. Cover and simmer slowly for about 1 hour. Remove the chickens; cool until they are comfortable to handle, then remove the skin. Remove meat from bones. Return bones to kettle and continue simmering another 30 minutes to extract all flavor. Place a large strainer over a bowl and strain the soup through it. Let the fat rise to the surface and, with a large shallow spoon, carefully skim it off. Dice the chicken meat. (You may save half of it for use in salads or creamed chicken.) Return the chicken meat to the broth. Cool quickly, pour into foil-lined bowls or pans and freeze. This makes 5 quarts broth and meat.

To serve: For each pint of the soup and chicken meat, cook ¼ cup fine noodles, alphabets, or other pasta in boiling salted water. Drain. Put frozen soup into the pan and heat gently until hot enough to serve, then add noodles, etc. Two tablespoons regular or 3 tablespoons precooked rice may be used. Add additional salt and pepper to taste.

To serve as Creamed Chicken: Thaw and heat 1 pint of the soup and chicken meat. Melt 4 tablespoons butter in a saucepan. Stir in 4 tablespoons flour and cook gently for 3 minutes. Remove from heat and place strainer over pan. Pour broth from chicken into butter-flour mixture. Stir vigorously and return to heat. Cook until thickened. Add ½ cup light or heavy cream and the chicken meat. Taste; add additional salt, pepper and a tablespoon of sherry wine. Sautéed mushrooms and/or chopped pimento may also be added. Toasted slivered almonds make a nice garnish. This makes 2 to 3 servings.

Chicken backs and necks are often sold very inexpensively. A supply of these trimmings—giblets as well—can be accumulated in the freezer, since chicken is a food frequently served. When time permits, make up a supply of your own chicken broth.

CHICKEN BROTH

*3 pounds chicken backs
   and necks
4 quarts water
1 teaspoon salt
2 onions, each stuck with
   a clove*

*1 leek (if available)
3 cloves garlic
4 stalks celery with
   leaves
5 peppercorns*

Wash chicken and put in a kettle with the water and salt. Bring slowly to a boil, skimming as needed. When foam ceases to rise, add vegetables and seasonings. Cook slowly 3 to 4 hours. Remove bones and vegetables. Wring out a square of cheesecloth in cold water and place in a large strainer over a large bowl. Ladle the broth into the strainer. Cool, chill and remove the fat that rises to the top. Pour into foil-lined bowls or pans and freeze. This makes 2½ to 3 quarts.

FRENCH ONION SOUP (6 servings)

2 tablespoons butter	*1 quart beef broth*
2 large onions, thinly	*3 cups water*
sliced	*Salt and pepper*
2 teaspoons flour	*Croutons*

Melt butter in a skillet, add onions and cook very slowly until onions are golden. Stir in flour and when blended add beef broth and water. Cook, stirring, until slightly thickened, then simmer for 10 to 15 minutes. Season to taste. Serve sprinkled with croutons.

French Onion Soup Gratinée: Follow recipe for French Onion Soup. Spread 6 thick slices of French bread with butter, place on foil and sprinkle with grated Parmesan or dry Swiss cheese. Brown under broiler. Serve soup with bread slices floating on top. Or pour soup into ovenproof tureen or ovenproof individual bowls, float the cheese-sprinkled bread slices on top and brown under broiler.

This is a fine last performance for the ham-end and bone which you've providently frozen for just such a use.

COUNTRY PEA SOUP BASE (16 servings)

Ham and bone	*1 carrot, chopped*
4 cups of split green peas	*½ cup chopped celery*
2 medium-size onions,	*Bay leaf*
chopped	*1 teaspoon salt*

Place ham and bone in large kettle with other ingredients and 4 quarts of water. Cover and simmer slowly 3 hours. If there is meat on the ham bone, remove meat from bone (discarding fat) after first hour so that it will not be overcooked. Remove bone and bay leaf from soup. Dice meat and add. Cool quickly; pour into foil-lined bowls or pans. Freeze. This should make about 3 quarts of very thick pea soup which may be diluted with 2 quarts or more of bouillon or water. To serve: Heat the frozen soup very gently;

add your own or canned beef broth or water to make a desired consistency. Season to taste.

Cream of Split Pea Soup: Milk and cream may be added, instead of beef bouillon. This makes a very creamy pea soup. Delectable served with crisp, buttery croutons floating on top.

Split Pea Soup with Frankfurters: For a very hearty meal, slice frankfurters into the soup after thawing and diluting; simmer for 2 to 3 minutes.

Black Bean Soup: This is another excellent soup to prepare ahead and have in the freezer. It is made exactly like Split Pea Soup; however, the beans must be soaked overnight since they have rather tough skins. After the mixture has been cooked it is best to put it through a food mill rather than a strainer. When serving Black Bean Soup, dilute it with beef broth or water and when hot, add a very generous amount of medium-dry Sherry.

Lentil Soup: Prepare this like Split Pea Soup. Remove bay leaf before freezing. To serve, heat slowly, adding water or beef broth to make desired consistency. People enjoy this soup with a little vinegar or lemon juice poured into each bowl of the soup at table.

LEEK AND POTATO SOUP BASE *(12 servings)*

4 tablespoons butter or margarine
2 cups chopped leek (use only the white part)
1 cup chopped onions
6 cups water
1 teaspoon salt
4 medium-size potatoes, diced
½ teaspoon each: thyme, rosemary

Melt the butter or margarine in a kettle. Add the leeks and onions; cook gently until soft but not brown. Add water and salt; bring to a boil, then add potatoes and herbs. Cover. Cook 15 to 20 minutes or until the potatoes are tender. Cool quickly; pour into foil-lined bowls or containers. Freeze. Makes about 2 quarts of soup which can be diluted with about ½ as much milk and cream. To serve: Heat gently, adding milk, a little cream, butter, salt and pepper to make a thick soup consistency. Serve with sprinkling of chopped chives.

Here are two fine ways to use up the tomatoes that suddenly ripen all at once in the garden.

TOMATO SOUP BASE *(10 servings)*

> *4 tablespoons butter or*
> *margarine*
> *1 onion, chopped*
> *1 carrot, chopped*
> *2 stalks celery, chopped*
> *1 leek, chopped (if*
> *available)*
> *1 clove garlic*
>
> *8 tablespoons flour*
> *12 large fresh tomatoes*
> *(1½ quarts chopped)*
> *1 teaspoon salt*
> *6 peppercorns*
> *1 tablespoon sugar*
> *1 quart chicken broth*

Melt butter or margarine in a large kettle. Add onion, carrot, celery, leek and garlic; cook slowly until golden brown. Stir in flour, blending well, add remaining ingredients. Cook, stirring, until the mixture boils. Cover. Continue cooking very slowly for 1 hour, stirring occasionally to prevent scorching. Rub through a fine sieve or food mill. Cool quickly. Pour into foil-lined bowls or containers and freeze. This makes about 2 quarts of thick tomato purée, which can be diluted with about ¼ as much milk and cream. To serve, heat gently, diluting with hot milk and cream. Add additional salt and pepper to taste. Serve with chopped parsley or chives, or a spoonful of whipped cream.

TOMATO BOUILLON BASE *(12 servings)*

> *14 large tomatoes (about*
> *2 quarts chopped)*
> *3 to 4 carrots*
> *3 to 4 onions*
> *4 to 5 leeks* OR
> *10 small onions*
> *1 bunch celery*
>
> *1 quart boiling water*
> *1 teaspoon salt*
> *Several sprigs fresh*
> *thyme*
> *Handful fresh basil*
> *1 tablespoon sugar*

Put all ingredients except sugar into a large kettle. Cover and cook slowly 2 hours; add more water as it cooks away to maintain original amount. Strain through a coarse sieve. Caramelize sugar by mixing with 2 tablespoons water and cooking until syrup is brown. Pour some of the bouillon over it and, when dissolved, add to remaining bouillon. Makes about 2 quarts. Cool, pour into foil-lined bowls or containers and freeze. To serve: Add ¼ as much beef broth or canned beef bouillon. Heat, adding additional salt and pepper to taste. Top with chives, parsley, or sour cream.

BOSTON FISH CHOWDER BASE   *(12 servings)*

3 to 4 pounds cod
1 quart water
1 teaspoon salt
4 tablespoons butter or
   margarine
3 medium-size onions,
   sliced or chopped

3 cups sliced or diced
   potatoes
¼ teaspoon each: thyme,
   rosemary
Generous grating of
   pepper

Cut the cod in convenient-size pieces and place it in a large kettle with water and salt. Cover. Cook gently until it begins to flake from bone. Lift out carefully; cool until it can be handled. Separate flesh from skin and bones, leaving fish in 1-inch pieces. Return bones to the kettle, cover. Simmer 10 minutes longer, then strain through a coarse strainer. There should be a quart or more of fish liquid. Rinse the kettle, then add butter and onions. Partially cover and cook the onions until they are tender but not brown. Add fish liquid, potatoes and seasonings. Cover and cook gently until potatoes are tender. Add the fish and bring just to a boil to blend the flavors. Cool, pour into foil-lined bowl or containers and freeze. This makes about 2 quarts of chowder base which may be diluted with about ½ the amount of fresh or evaporated milk. To serve: Heat gently, adding rich milk to make consistency of chowder. Add salt and pepper to taste. Sprinkle each serving with paprika.

Good to know: Traditionally, chowder is made with salt pork. For freezing, butter or margarine is better. You may fry diced salt pork until crisp and use to garnish the chowder when serving, if desired. Chowder may be made from frozen fish fillets. You will not have to contend with bones. It will be very good, but not quite as flavorful as when made with the whole fish.

CLAM CHOWDER BASE   *(8 servings)*

3 tablespoons butter or
   margarine
1 large onion, chopped
2 cups water
3 cups diced potatoes

2 10½-ounce cans
   minced clams
½ teaspoon salt
Grating of pepper
½ teaspoon thyme

Melt butter in kettle, add onions and cook slowly until soft but not brown. Add water; bring to a boil and add potatoes. Cover. Cook slowly about 20 minutes or until potatoes are done. Add clams, bring back to the boil and add salt, pepper, thyme. Cool quickly. Pour into foil-lined bowl or pan. Freeze. Makes about 3 pints of chowder base. To serve: Heat gently, adding 1 cup fresh or evaporated milk and salt and pepper to taste to each pint of chowder. Add a teaspoon of butter to each serving and accompany with pilot crackers or large old fashioned crackers.

Good to know: If you are lucky enough to have fresh clams, substitute 2 cups chopped fresh clams for the canned.

MANHATTAN CLAM CHOWDER BASE   *(12 servings)*

4 tablespoons butter or margarine
1 cup diced onions
3 cups diced peeled potatoes
½ cup diced celery
1 cup diced scraped carrots
2 cups canned tomatoes
1 teaspoon salt
½ teaspoon thyme
2 cups fresh clams out of the shell, OR
2 10½-ounce cans minced clams

Melt the butter in a good-size saucepan and add the onions. Cook gently until tender but not brown. Add fresh and canned vegetables, seasonings. Cover and continue cooking gently until just tender. If clams are fresh, put through a food chopper or cut in small pieces. Add clams with juice. Bring just to a boil. Cool quickly and pour into foil-lined bowls or containers and freeze. This makes about 2 quarts of chowder base. To serve: Add 1 cup canned tomato juice to each pint of the frozen base. Heat gently, adding additional seasonings and a little butter to taste.

CREAM OF MUSHROOM SOUP BASE   *(16 servings)*

½ cup butter or margarine
1 cup finely chopped onions
½ cup flour
2 quarts hot homemade chicken broth OR
1 large can (1 quart 14 ounces)
½ teaspoon each: rosemary, thyme
Few sprigs parsley
1 teaspoon salt
2 pounds fresh or frozen mushrooms
4 tablespoons butter
1 teaspoon lemon juice

Melt ½ cup butter in a large saucepan; add onions and cook until tender but not brown. Stir in flour, blending thoroughly. Remove pan from heat and add the hot broth, stirring until well combined. Return to heat; stir and cook until smooth and thickened. Add seasonings. Wipe mushrooms with soft cloth or, if sandy, rinse quickly and dry on a soft towel. Remove the choice caps— about 1 cup. Chop stems and remainder of mushrooms very coarsely. Add to thickened broth. Cover; cook very gently, stirring occasionally, about 30 minutes. Slice reserved caps. Melt 4 tablespoons butter in skillet; cook sliced caps about 10 minutes, sprinkling with the lemon juice to keep them light in color. Strain the thickened broth and mushroom mixture through a food mill or strainer, pressing to get all flavor from the mushrooms. Add cooked mushroom caps; reheat just to the simmer point. Cool quickly; pour into foil-lined pans or bowls. Freeze. This makes about 2 quarts of mushroom soup base, which may be diluted with an equal amount of milk and light cream. To serve: Reheat gently, adding milk and cream and stirring to blend. Add salt and pepper to taste.

SOUTH AFRICAN LOBSTER BISQUE BASE *(10 servings)*

6 4-ounce rock lobster   *2 tablespoons snipped*
   tails   *parsley*
¾ cup butter   *¼ teaspoon celery salt*
½ cup flour   *½ teaspoon salt*
2 quarts hot milk   *¼ teaspoon nutmeg*
1 medium onion, grated

Cut frozen rock lobster tails in 1-inch pieces. Melt ¼ cup of the butter in a saucepan and add the lobster tails. Partially cover pan and cook for 6 to 10 minutes. Lift out the lobster to a plate and let it cool. Add remaining butter to the pan and melt. Stir in flour and cook for 3 minutes over low heat. Remove the pan from the heat and add the milk, stirring. Add onion, parsley, seasonings; return to heat and cook, stirring, until thickened and smooth. Remove lobster meat from the shell, dice, and add to mixture in saucepan. Bring just to the simmer point, then cool quickly. Pour into foil-lined containers or bowls and freeze. This makes 2 quarts of bisque which may be diluted with 1 pint of heavy cream. To serve: Reheat gently; to each pint of base add ½ cup cream, salt and white pepper.

SOPHISTICATED COLD SOUPS

If you want to raise your guests' eyebrows, begin a meal—particularly on a very hot day—with icy cold Vichyssoise or Crème St. Germain. Or make it a sparkling jellied soup topped with *fines herbes*—finely chopped parsley, chives and tarragon—or just chopped parsley and a wedge of lemon.

The basic stocks for Vichyssoise or Crème St. Germain can be frozen and, after defrosting, finished with the milk and cream as directed.

VICHYSSOISE BASE (12 servings)

4 tablespoons butter or margarine	1 quart hot chicken broth or water
3 leeks, white parts, chopped	6 cups thinly sliced potatoes
1 medium onion, chopped	2 cups hot milk

Melt butter in a large kettle, add leeks (if unobtainable replace with 2 onions) and onion; cook slowly until soft but not brown. Stir occasionally. Add broth or water, potatoes and salt. Cover. Cook gently 30 minutes or until potatoes are very soft. Rub through food mill or strainer. Combine with milk and bring back to a boil, stirring to prevent scorching. Strain again through fine sieve. Cool quickly, stirring occasionally; pour into foil-lined pans or bowls. Freeze. Makes about 2 quarts of Vichyssoise base. To serve: Heat base gently until it is hot but not boiling. If you wish it very smooth, force it through a fine sieve once more or whirl in a blender. Add 1 cup heavy cream, salt and white pepper to taste, to each pint of warm base. Blend well, chill thoroughly. Serve in chilled bowls with topping of chopped chives or *fines herbes*.

CRÈME ST. GERMAIN GLACÉE (9 servings)

2 tablespoons butter	3 cups fresh or frozen peas
1½ cups chopped onions and leeks (OR all onion)	1 cup diced potatoes
1 quart chicken broth or water	1 teaspoon salt

Melt butter in a large kettle, add leeks and onions. Partially cover, cook slowly until soft but not brown. Add broth or water and peas; bring to a boil, add potatoes, salt. Cook covered 20 minutes or until peas and potatoes are very soft. Strain through food mill, then through fine strainer. Cool, then spoon into foil-lined bowls or pans. Freeze. This makes 3 pints of base. To serve: Thaw and heat the base until hot but not boiling. Again force through a fine sieve or whirl in blender; add 1 cup heavy cream for each pint of base, salt and white pepper to taste. Blend thoroughly, chill again. Serve in icy cold cups or bowls with sprinkling of chopped fresh tarragon.

JELLIED MADRILÈNE *(6 servings)*

6 cups chicken broth
*2 cups canned tomato
   juice*
2 tablespoons gelatin

¼ cup water
Salt
*2 egg whites, lightly
   beaten*

Combine chicken broth and tomato juice in a large kettle and heat to the boiling point. Soften gelatin in water and add. Add salt to taste. Stir in egg whites and bring slowly to a boil, stirring gently all the time. Stop stirring when boiling point is reached; reduce heat so that mixture barely bubbles, or put kettle where it will keep very hot for 30 minutes. Line a large strainer with cheesecloth wrung out in cold water; place over a bowl. Use a cup or ladle to dip out the soup and strain through the cheesecloth. Cover bowl with foil, then chill thoroughly until mixture has a quivery, jellied texture. This may be kept in the refrigerator 1 week.

Good to know: If canned chicken broth is used, the large can (1 quart 14 ounces) holds 7 cups. Add to it any leftover trimmings from chicken—the necks, etc.—that you may have in the freezer, along with a stalk of celery with leaves, a small onion stuck with a clove, 4 peppercorns and a small bay leaf. Simmer for 30 minutes, until reduced by about 1 cup. Strain and use in the recipe.

GAZPACHO *(6 to 8 servings)*

*4 tomatoes, peeled and
   seeded*
*2 cucumbers, peeled and
   seeded*
*1 green pepper,
   seeds removed*
2 cloves garlic, crushed
*1 sweet red onion,
   chopped*

*½ cup parsley sprigs
   without coarse stems*
4 eggs
2 teaspoons salt
4 drops Tabasco
¼ cup wine vinegar
¼ cup olive oil

As you prepare the vegetables, cut them in small pieces and combine in a bowl with the eggs, salt and Tabasco. Divide into 3 or 4 loads and whirl in the blender a few minutes. Or put through the food mill. Combine with the vinegar and oil, cover with foil and chill for 2 to 3 hours.

Get ready a relish dish with these accompaniments:

2 cups garlic croutons

1 large tomato, seeded and diced

1 green pepper, membrane and seeds removed, diced

1 cucumber, peeled, seeded and diced

1 cup scallions or mild red onions, chopped

Cover the relish dish with foil and chill. To serve, put an ice cube in the center of each cold bowl, pour in the soup. Pass the relishes to be spooned into the soup.

SOUP GARNISHES

Prepare these garnishes on days when fresh herbs are available in the markets or your own garden, and when you have time to spare for some simple little extras that will help give the foods you serve that out-of-the-ordinary aura.

Wrap these garnishings in foil, making little packets each of which contains the amount needed to top the number of cups or bowls of soup you usually serve. Label the packets with a magic marker and bind 6 or more together with a rubber band. They'll keep for 6 months or longer.

To use, remove a packet and run cold water over it for a minute; then use as you would the fresh item. They are great for soups . . . for many other dishes, also.

Chopped herbs: Parsley, chives and all fresh herbs such as thyme, rosemary, tarragon, sage, and those summer annuals, chervil and basil, can be chopped and packed in little foil packets. Simply chop the herb with a sharp knife on a board or use scissors to snip into small bits.

Fine herbs: This is the French mixture of chives, parsley, tarragon and thyme or chervil. Little packets of these herbs, already mixed, are wonderfully good for topping soup, for adding to omelets and sauces, and for seasoning many dishes.

Croutons: Remove the crusts from bread that is several days old. Cut into ¼-inch cubes. Heat butter or margarine in a skillet and brown the cubes, stirring and turning them until they are brown all over. Drain on paper towels. They may be refrigerated, or frozen in foil packets. Although it isn't necessary, they are most appetizing if you open the foil packet and pop the croutons into the oven to heat for 5 minutes before topping soup.

Garlic croutons, herb-flavored croutons: Add a few snips of garlic or fresh or dried herbs to butter or margarine when browning cubes. Or sprinkle the croutons with garlic salt or dried herbs just before use. The croutons may be browned in bacon fat for topping hearty pea and bean soups.

Toasted slivered almonds: Brown slivered almonds on a sheet of foil or foil pie pan in a 350°F oven. Stir and turn them once or twice and remove before they are too deep in color. Or brown them in butter or margarine in a skillet on the surface of the range. Cool and pack in foil packets.

Whipped cream rosettes: Add pinch of paprika or herbs to cream and whip. Drop by spoonfuls on foil, swirling to make an attractive shape. Freeze until firm, then pack in a foil-lined box. Take out as many as needed, resealing the foil each time.

Magic with Meat

Magic
with Meat

***Rich, juicy, tender . . . with savory gourmet specialties
that you didn't know you had time for***

Storing meats in the refrigerator and freezer: Supermarkets display an enormous variety of meats already cut, and ready for cooking. Many will also cut an extra-thick steak or bone a roast for you. If you want special attention, try to shop when the market is not crowded, or place your order ahead of time.

Since meat is the most expensive item on your food budget, it should be carefully purchased. Buy the specials, and when certain cuts that your family enjoys are on sale, buy them in quantity and freeze them.

Proper care and storage of meats are important, as they quickly lose flavor and freshness and some of their nutritional value when exposed to heat or air. Here are suggestions to guide you.

Refrigerator storage: Remove paper or transparent wrappings from fresh meats, place on a tray or plate and cover loosely with foil. Do not seal airtight. Smoked meats, sliced sandwich meats, frankfurters, sausage, corned beef may be left in their own moisture-proof wraps. Store all meats in the coolest part of the refrigerator. Don't keep chopped meats or liver longer than 2 days. Other fresh meats may be kept 2 to 4 days, smoked and sandwich meats 5 to 7 days.

Freezer Storage: Meats must have good moisture-vaporproof wrapping or they will dry out, discolor, lose flavor and vitamin content. The usual paper or transparent wrapping in which meat comes from the market is inadequate.

Heavy Duty Reynolds Wrap provides excellent protection. See page 182 for information important for all freezer-bound food; and following are specific wrapping directions for the successful storage of home-frozen meats.

1. Place meat in the center of a suitable-size sheet of heavy duty foil. If there are sharp or protruding bones, pad these with small folds of foil.

In color picture: Flavor-Baked Ham

2. Bring long ends of foil together above the meat and fold over and over, creasing firmly until the fold rests on the surface of the meat.

3. Mold or press the foil to conform to the shape of the meat, pressing out the air.

4. Turn in corners of the still-open ends and fold, creasing lightly.

Package labeling: It's easy to forget what's in a package, so don't omit labeling. Use a strip of freezer tape (masking tape is the same product). Mark the contents and date on the tapes, using a soft lead pencil or child's colored crayon. Or use a felt-tipped marking pen (sold at variety and stationery stores). Such a pen will write directly on foil, but is not quite as easy to read.

Some hams and shoulders come in foil wrappings, but all smoked meats, sausages, and frankfurters with other types of wrappings should be given an extra wrap of foil. Because of high salt and fat content, these foods lose flavor rapidly.

Meat patties and hamburgers may be seasoned and formed into the size and shape you like. Package them in amounts needed for one meal. Separate patties with double squares of foil so they may be taken apart easily. When packaging several steaks or chops together, separate them with double-folded piece of foil.

Cooking frozen meat: It is best to thaw roasts and thick cuts before cooking. Remove from freezer a day or more ahead. Do not unwrap; place on a pan on refrigerator shelf. A 5-inch-thick roast will take 3 days to thaw on the refrigerator shelf. Meat may be thawed at room temperature in less time but will lose more juice.

If you do roast from the frozen state, try to select a roast not over 3 inches in diameter. Allow about ⅓ to ½ longer than usual, and use a meat thermometer to determine doneness, since it's difficult to give precise time for frozen roasts. Insert the thermometer when meat has been in the oven about ⅔ of the time. The outer part of the roast is apt to be quite well done when the center is still rare—which is an advantage in some families.

Pot roasts and other meats to be cooked by braising should be thawed before cooking.

Steaks and chops may be broiled from the frozen state very successfully. It's often the only way of broiling a thin steak rare.

Oven defrosting: Ovens that maintain a very low temperature (140° to 180°F) are sometimes recommended for thawing frozen meats. They are chiefly useful for thawing chopped meats, meat cut for stew, etc. Thaw only until the meat can be handled easily.

How long will meat keep in the freezer? This depends on the type of freezer. Freezers in the tops of refrigerators usually maintain a temperature of 10° to 15°F above zero. Meat should not be kept in them for longer than one month.

Combination refrigerator-freezers vary; some maintain zero in their freezing compartments and so state in their use-and-care manuals. Separate freezers, designed for freezing only, maintain zero or lower. At zero or lower, meats keep flavor and freshness much longer. The following chart, prepared by USDA's Agricultural Research Service, gives recommended storage periods for home-frozen meats.

Product	Storage Period (months)	Product	Storage Period (months)
BEEF:		PORK, cured:	
Ground meat	2-3	Bacon	Less than 1
Roasts	8-12	Ham	1-2
Steaks	8-12	PORK, fresh:	
		Chops	3-4
LAMB:		Roasts	4-8
Chops	3-4	Sausage	1-2
Ground meat	2-3		
Roasts	8-12	VEAL:	
		Cutlets, chops	3-4
		Ground meat	2-3
		Roasts	4-8
For best quality use shorter storage time. Store at 0°F.			

Broiling: Everyone agrees that broiled meats are delicious and healthful. But many cooks avoid broiling because they dislike the messy clean-up afterward, because of smoke in the kitchen, or because they do not get beautifully browned meat done to their taste.

For good broiling, meats must rest on a rack above a pan. Melting fat *must* drain away from the meat into the bottom of the pan. Smokeless broiler pans come with modern ranges. These have an upper rack which holds the meat and is designed to protect the melted fat in the bottom pan from full broiler heat. Generally, the rack has wide bars with narrow slits or openings for the fat to drain through.

To avoid messy clean-up after broiling: line the pan of the broiler with Heavy Duty Reynolds Wrap, letting it extend up sides of pan. Place the rack in position and the meat on the rack. If the rack is troublesome to clean, it may be lined as well, but be sure to mold

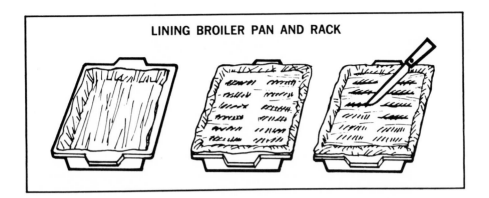

LINING BROILER PAN AND RACK

foil to shape of rack and *cut slits or openings* to conform with those in the rack, so that fat will drain away.

Set thermostat at "broil." Light or turn on the broiler and preheat for 4 to 5 minutes. Place the pan with meat under the flame or electric unit, allowing 3 to 4 inches between the surface of the meat and the heat. Leave oven or broiler door ajar so moisture may escape and so broiler flame or unit stays at full heat. As soon as first side is brown, turn and brown second side. Consult your range instruction book for specific broiling directions for your range.

TIMETABLE FOR BROILING MEATS

Cut	Thickness	Approx. Total Minutes		
		Rare	**Med.**	**Well**
Steak	1"	10-12	14-16	20-25
	1½"	14-16	18-20	25-30
	2"	20-25	30-35	40-45
Hamburgers	¾"	8	12	15
Lamb Chops				
1 Rib	¾"	—	10-12	14-15
Double Rib	1½"	—	18-20	22-25
Ham Slice	¾"	—	—	13-14
Bacon	Regular	—	—	4-5
	Thick	—	—	6-7

Broiling small amounts of meat: Small smokeless broiler pans just the right size for a few chops or a small steak are available at stores selling aluminum cookware. They may be lined with heavy duty foil.

Good to know about broiling: Trim fat from meat, leaving not much more than ¼ inch around outside of steak or chops. Trim fat from center. This will lessen smoke during broiling. Large amounts of fat left on meat do not add to its flavor. Gash fat at intervals on large steaks, chops, ham slices, to prevent curling and keep meat flat.

Broiling frozen steaks, chops: Don't defrost unless more than 1½ inches thick. Broil right from the frozen state, placing the broiler pan 2 inches farther away from heat than usual and allowing 5 to 10 minutes longer, depending on the thickness of the meat. Thin steaks are more easily done rare and meats often seem more juicy when broiled right from the freezer. Test by cutting edge with a sharp knife.

SPRING BROILER DINNER   *(4 servings)*

> 4 lamb chops, cut 1 inch
>   thick
> 4 potatoes, canned or
>   home cooked
> Melted butter or
>   margarine

> Salt and pepper
> 4 canned cling peach
>   halves, drained
> 4 teaspoons
>   currant or mint jelly

Trim fat from chops. Line broiler pan with foil. Arrange chops and potatoes on broiler rack. If potatoes are small, place them in a foil pan prepared by turning up edges of a double-thick square of heavy duty foil and mitering corners. If they are large, cut in half lengthwise. Brush potatoes with melted butter and season. Place under preheated broiler flame or unit and broil, turning chops and seasoning them on the second side. Turn potatoes several times. Five minutes before chops are done, place peaches on broiler rack, brush with melted butter and fill centers with jelly. Serve garnished with watercress.

PATTY CAKE CHOPPED STEAK DINNER   *(6 to 8 servings)*

> 2 pounds chopped chuck
>   or round
> 2 teaspoons monosodium
>   glutamate
> Salt, black pepper
> Melted butter
> 2 packages frozen lima
>   beans with cheese
>   sauce

> Grated cheese
> 4 firm tomatoes, cut in
>   half
> 4 medium-size cooked
>   potatoes, sliced
>   lengthwise

Break up meat with fork in large mixing bowl. Sprinkle monosodium glutamate, 2 teaspoons salt and a grinding of pepper over meat. Toss with fork just enough to blend. Shape into an 8-inch patty about 1½ inches thick. Handle as little as possible. Line bottom of broiler pan. Cut a circle of heavy duty foil same size and shape as patty. Place on rack of broiler pan. Punch a few holes through foil. Place meat patty on foil. Brush top with melted butter. Place under a preheated broiler and broil until first side is nicely browned. Slip a large spatula under the foil and turn meat patty (grasp edge of foil with fingers to help). Remove foil. Brush second side with butter and broil. While first side browns, prepare frozen limas according to package directions. Pour into small foil pan and sprinkle with cheese. When you turn patty, place limas, tomatoes and potatoes on broiler pan. Brush tomatoes and potatoes with butter and sprinkle with seasonings and cheese. Broil meat and vegetables until brown.

STEAK AU POIVRE
Line the broiler pan as directed. Sprinkle a 2 to 3 inch thick flank or sirloin steak very liberally with fresh cracked pepper. (Place peppercorns on board, a few at a time, crack by rolling with rolling pin.) Press in with the back of a knife. Let stand 10 to 15 minutes. Preheat broiler. Line broiler pan. Place the steak on rack of broiler pan and place under broiler. Broil quickly until brown, but rare, turning once.

Remove broiler pan from range and transfer steak to a warm wooden plank. Skim off excess fat from drippings; pick up foil and pour drippings over steak. Season with salt.

Flambé the steak as follows: Warm ½ cup cognac or brandy in a small saucepan, pour over steak and light with a match. Spoon burning brandy and steak juices over steak. When the flame dies down, carve the steak with a very sharp knife on the slant, in thin ¼-inch slices. Serve slices with the brandy-flavored juices spooned over.

Great go-withs: Delicious with foil-baked potatoes, vegetables, and crusty French bread to sop up the juices.

PAN FRYING AND BROWNING
This is a good method for preparing pork chops, hamburgers, bacon, thinly sliced liver, veal cutlets and veal chops. Many recipes for stews, ragouts and casseroles call for first browning the meat.

You'll find it helpful to place a good-size sheet of Reynolds Wrap —either Heavy Duty or Standard, whichever fits best—partially over your skillet. Shape it tent-fashion, to catch sputters, keep the range clean. Don't cover the skillet tightly—this prevents good browning. Flatten out the foil after browning, and press tight against skillet to continue cooking and to braise meat such as pork chops or veal. Foil makes a fine skillet cover during braising, since it holds in just enough moisture to finish the cooking.

MEAT TENDERIZERS

Both seasoned and unseasoned tenderizers help make less tender cuts of meat more palatable. Sprinkle over surfaces and pierce at 1-inch intervals with a long-pronged fork. Let meat stand at room temperature for 1 hour, or cover loosely with Reynolds Wrap and refrigerate overnight. Don't salt, as tenderizers contain salt.

ROASTING MEATS WITH REYNOLDS WRAP

Is it a good idea to roast meat in foil or isn't it? This is a hotly debated question. Meat industry home economists do not recommend it, but some homemakers like the type of roast it produces. And gourmet cooks devise wonderful recipes for less tender cuts roasted in foil with wine, herbs and other delightful seasonings.

Foil roasting produces a flavorful, juicy roast, much like one cooked in the old–fashioned double roaster. It helps to keep the oven clean, too!

Meats are first browned with the foil open in a hot oven. After browning, the foil is very loosely closed—not sealed airtight. For true roasted flavor some of the steam must escape. Here is a step-by-step guide for roasting meat in foil:

1. Preheat oven to very hot (450°F).
2. Arrange a sheet of Heavy Duty Reynolds Wrap, large enough to completely wrap meat, in a shallow roasting pan.
3. Place meat in center, fold edges of foil close to the pan, and roast for 30 to 40 minutes, or until meat is nicely browned. Add seasonings, diced onion, celery and carrots during last 10 minutes.
5. Close foil as follows: bring two opposite ends of foil up over meat, overlapping them 2 to 3 inches. Close open ends by turning up the foil. *Wrap loosely; do not seal airtight.*

6. Insert meat thermometer, if used, right through foil into thickest part of meat, without touching bone.

7. Roast according to time chart.

8. Open the foil again during the last 10 minutes of roasting time, if desired.

FOIL-ROASTING TIMETABLE FOR FRESH MEATS
Oven Temperature 425-450°F

Type of Roast	Weight	Approximate Cooking Time in Hours			Meat-Thermometer Temperature
		RARE	MED.	WELL	
BEEF Standing					
ribs	4-5 pounds	1¼	1½	1¾	140-170°
	6-8 pounds	1½	2	2½	140-170°
Rolled rib					
or sirloin	3-4 pounds	1½	2	2½	140-170°
	5-6 pounds	1¾	2½	3	140-170°
LAMB					
Leg	6-7 pounds		2-2¼		170-180°
Half leg	3-4 pounds		1¾-2		170-180°
VEAL					
Leg	5-8 pounds			2¼-3	170°
Rolled					
shoulder	4-6 pounds			2-3	170°
PORK, fresh					
Loin	3-6 pounds			2-2½	185°
Fresh ham	10-12 pounds			3½-4	185°

OPEN-PAN MEAT ROASTING

Most people prefer to roast meat without completely wrapping it in foil. To avoid a messy cleaning job, the pan may be lined with Heavy Duty Reynolds Wrap, smoothing it to conform to the shape of the pan.

If, after the meat has been roasting for some time and is browned sufficiently, there is a danger of overbrowning, or if fat spatters, a "tent" of foil may be placed over the meat. It should fit very loosely to allow for circulation of heat under the foil. Use the temperature and time you are accustomed to. Meat industry home economists recommend the following:

TIMETABLE FOR OPEN-PAN ROASTING

Cut	Weight	Oven Temperature Constant	Meat Thermometer Temperature	Approximate Time Per Pound
	Pounds	Degrees F		Minutes
BEEF				
Standing ribs	6-8	325	140 (rare)	23-25
			160 (med.)	27-30
			170 (well)	32-35
Standing rib (1 rib)	2	350	140 (rare)	33
			160 (med.)	45
			170 (well)	50
Rolled rib	5-7	325	140 (rare)	32
			160 (med.)	38
			170 (well)	48
Rolled rump (high quality)	4-6	325	150-170	25-30
Sirloin tip (high quality)	3½-4	325	150-170	35-40
PORK, fresh				
Loin, center cut	3-5	350	170	30-35
half	5-7	350	170	35-40
ends	2-3	350	170	40-45
Picnic shoulder	4-6	350	185	30-35
boned and rolled	3-5	350	185	40-45
cushion-style	3-5	350	185	35-40
Boston butt	4-6	350	185	45-50
Fresh ham, whole	10-14	350	185	25-30
LAMB				
Leg	5-8	325	175-180	30-35
Shoulder (bone in)	4-6	325	175-180	30-35
rolled	3-5	325	175-180	40-45
cushion-style	3-5	325	175-180	30-35
VEAL				
Leg	5-8	325	170	25-35
Loin	4-6	325	170	30-35
Rib (rack)	3-5	325	170	35-40
Rolled shoulder	4-6	325	170	40-45

ROAST LEG OF LAMB, OLD WORLD STYLE
(10 or more servings)

6 to 8 pound leg of lamb
1 clove garlic
1 teaspoon salt
¼ teaspoon pepper
¼ teaspoon rosemary
1 tablespoon olive or
  salad oil
1 tablespoon honey
1 carrot, cut up

1 onion, quartered
½ cup dry red wine OR
¼ cup each lemon juice
  and bland canned
  fruit juice
Whole carrots
New potatoes
Cornstarch

Trim fat from lamb. Arrange a large sheet of heavy duty foil in a shallow pan and place lamb in center. Fold foil close to meat. Crush garlic into salt, add pepper, rosemary and olive oil and honey. Rub this mixture over the meat. Sprinkle carrot and onion around meat.

Place in a 450°F oven and brown the meat. This takes about 30 minutes. Reduce heat to 375°F. Slide the pan out of the oven and pour the wine or fruit juice over the lamb. Take the ends of folded foil on the long sides of the lamb and bring up over the meat, overlapping about 3 inches. Close the foil at either end by turning it up, so juice cannot run out. *Wrap loosely; do not seal.*

Put the lamb back into the oven and roast for 1½ hours longer. At the end of this time, open the foil on the lamb and fold it back. Using a spoon, remove the fat in the drippings and remove onion and carrot. Baste the lamb with juice in the foil. Cook carrots and potatoes in boiling salted water during last half hour. Drain. Add potatoes and carrots to foil, basting these also. Return to oven for just a few minutes to glaze vegetables.

Lift meat and vegetables to serving platter. Pour drippings into a saucepan. Add boiling water to make desired amount of gravy. Thicken with a little cornstarch mixed with wine or fruit juice. Add salt and pepper to taste, simmer a few minutes and serve.

CROWN ROAST OF PORK, HOLIDAY STUFFING *(8 servings)*

Have butcher prepare the crown roast, telling him how many ribs you need. Allow 2 per person or 16 for a party of 8. He will tie 2 or 3 center sections of pork loin to form a circle, after he has trimmed away the meat from the ends of the ribs (called Frenching) and cut the backbone completely away to make carving easier.

Place roast in a foil-lined pan and rub all over with salt, pepper, thyme and marjoram. Cover each rib-end with a small piece of foil to prevent darkening or scorching. Cut a round of the foil a little larger than the center and fit it inside at the bottom. Roast in a 350°F preheated oven for 1½ hours. Remove from oven, fill center with stuffing, return to oven and cook another hour. Lift out to heated serving platter using a large, broad spatula.

Remove all fat from drippings. Pour in 3 cups dry white wine. Cook slowly, stirring to dissolve all browned juices. Mix 2 tablespoons cornstarch with ¼ cup additional wine and add; continue stirring until smooth and slightly thickened. Add additional salt and pepper to taste.

Remove foil from rib-ends of roast and replace with frills cut from foil. Garnish by alternating around the roast small white onions and brussels sprouts which have been cooked and then glazed with hot melted butter or margarine.

HOLIDAY STUFFING:

> ½ 7-ounce package
>   stuffing croutons
> ½ cup finely chopped
>   onions
> ½ cup butter

> 1 cup ready-to-use
>   mincemeat
> ½ to ¾ cup boiling water

Turn croutons into a bowl. Add the onions sautéed in the butter. Add the mincemeat and toss together with a fork. Rinse out skillet with water and add, moistening stuffing to desired consistency.

SAUCES AND GRAVIES . . . HOW TO MAKE THEM

Pan gravy: Often all that's necessary to serve with a roast are the juices that have formed during roasting. After removing meat to serving platter or carving board, carefully skim off all fat. Leave onions, celery, carrots, etc. that have been cooked with roast and add boiling water. (Or, to improve the flavor, use hot homemade or canned clear broth.) If pan has been lined with foil, pour liquids right into the foil. Tip pan and swish around to dissolve all browned juices. Pour into saucepan, add additional seasonings; simmer until reduced a little. Strain into sauceboat.

Thickened gravy: Remove all but 1 or 2 tablespoons of fat from the drippings. Stir in 2 level tablespoons of flour for each cup of liquid you expect to add. Cook flour-fat mixture over low heat for 3 to 4 minutes, then add boiling water or hot broth. Stir and cook until thickened and smooth. Add seasonings and strain. Finished gravy should be the consistency of unwhipped heavy cream.

Weight watchers' gravy: Remove all fat from drippings, add boiling water or broth. Heat to dissolve browned juices. Mix 2 tablespoons of flour with ¼ cup water for each cup of hot liquid (use wire whisk, or shake in small jar). Add to the hot liquid; stir and cook until thickened. Add seasonings.

Instant no-sift flour is an aid to making thickened gravies. Add cold water or broth to drippings, stir in the flour without premixing with water. It will blend readily with cold liquid. Simmer and season.

Wine sauces: When wine or vermouth has been used in roasting meat, cornstarch can be used to make a clear, delicious sauce. For each cup of liquid, mix 1 level tablespoon of cornstarch with 2 tablespoons wine or cold water; add to drippings and broth and cook as in weight watchers' gravy.

Mushroom gravy: Allow about 6 medium fresh or 1 6-ounce can mushrooms for 2 cups of gravy. Slice them or cut in quarters and sauté quickly in butter. Remove mushrooms, add flour to the butter remaining in pan and cook over low heat for 3 to 4 minutes. Add drippings and hot broth; stir and cook until thickened.

FOIL METHOD OF POT ROASTING

Cooking a pot roast in Heavy Duty Reynolds Wrap has several distinct advantages. You don't need grandmother's old-fashioned kettle. You can brown the meat under the broiler, an easy process that doesn't spatter fat. Or you can brown it in a skillet. Then the meat goes into a large piece of heavy duty foil, completely sealed, to cook without watching. All the wonderful meat juices and flavors of other ingredients added to the roast will be saved. And the meat will be deliciously tender, with the best gravy ever.

POT ROAST OF BEEF COUNTRY STYLE   *(8-10 servings)*

4 to 5 pound boneless pot roast
2 small onions, chopped
1 small carrot, diced
Small stalk of celery, diced

Salt and pepper
Bay leaf, parsley sprig
½ cup canned tomato sauce (optional)

Tear off enough heavy duty foil to completely wrap the roast and allow for flavoring vegetables. Place the foil on a shallow pan and place the meat in the center. Fold the foil up around the meat (so that it is not spread out) and place under broiler flame or unit. Brown, turning until all sides of the meat are browned fairly well. While the meat is browning, prepare the vegetables and add at the last, turning so they may brown slightly. (The meat and vegetables may be browned in a skillet, then placed on foil.) Turn down the heat and set oven thermostat for slow (275° to 300°F). Remove the meat from the broiler. Pour tomato sauce over, if desired—otherwise use no liquid. Add salt and freshly ground pepper, a little crumbled bay leaf, the parsley and other desired herbs. Close the foil, sealing all edges with a tight double fold to form an air-tight package. Place in oven in usual roasting position. Bake for 3 to 3½ hours. If longer time can be spared and the range maintains a low temperature accurately, it may be baked for 4 hours at 250°F. When baking time is finished, remove roast from oven and open foil. Transfer the meat to a hot platter.

Gravy: Pour the juices with vegetables into a saucepan and skim off fat. Let simmer until slightly reduced in amount. Taste and add additional seasonings, as desired. This gravy is so flavorful and rich, you will want to serve it as a sauce. It may also be thickened in the usual manner.

Beef à la Ritz: Brown pot roast as above; place meat in center of the foil. Substitute ½ pound fresh or one 6-ounce can of mushrooms, drained, for the carrots and celery in the above recipe. After browning, add a small clove of garlic crushed in the salt; pour ⅓ cup dry red wine over. Seal foil and bake as above.

VEGETABLES TO ACCOMPANY POT ROAST

Although it is quite possible to open the foil when cooking a pot roast and add vegetables 1 hour or more before it is done, it is easier and the vegetables have better color and more distinct flavor if they are cooked in a separate package.

Peel potatoes, small onions, carrots, parsnips—enough for the number of people to be served. Place them on one or two large pieces of heavy duty foil and sprinkle with salt, pepper and dot with butter. Sprinkle with 1 or 2 tablespoons of water. Seal the foil to make a tight package. Place package on a shallow pan and bake for 1½ hours at 300°F or bake it for 2 to 2½ hours at 250°F.

SUPER POT ROAST

(6 to 8 servings)

3 to 4 pound boneless   *1 envelope (1⅜ ounce)*
*   pot roast*   *onion soup mix*

Arrange a long sheet of heavy duty foil in a shallow pan and place the meat in the center. Sprinkle all sides of meat with onion soup mix. Bring long ends of foil up over meat and seal with double fold. Turn other ends up and seal in same way. Bake at 350°F 2½ to 3 hours or at 300°F 3½ to 4 hours. When done, open one end of package and pour juices into saucepan. Skim off excess fat and serve this broth as is, or thicken with mixture of flour and water.

SAVORY SWISS STEAK

(6 to 7 servings)

2½ to 3 pound boneless   *¼ pound fresh*
*   chuck steak*   *   mushrooms sliced* OR
1 1⅜-ounce envelope   *1 6-ounce can sliced*
*   onion soup mix*   *   mushrooms, drained*

Trim excess fat from meat. Place a long sheet of heavy duty foil on a shallow pan. Place meat in center and sprinkle all sides with the soup mix. Top with the mushrooms. Bring long ends of foil up over meat and seal with tight double fold. Turn up other ends and seal in same way. Bake at 350°F 2 to 2½ hours, or at 300°F 3 to 3½ hours. Serve with delicious sauce formed in the foil.

If Boeuf à la Mode is prepared in the real French manner, the meat is larded with long strips of fresh fat pork. Veal bones and a calf's foot are cooked with the meat also, to add substance to the sauce. But the dish is delicious without any of these bothersome steps. If you wish to use the bones, go ahead, but be sure to allow plenty of room in package and take care not to puncture the foil.

BOEUF A LA MODE

(8 to 10 servings)

4 to 5 pound boneless   *2 teaspoons thyme*
*   chuck or round roast*   *2 bay leaves*
Salt and pepper   *¼ cup minced parsley*
1 large onion, sliced   *2 cups red wine*
1 carrot, sliced   *¼ cup brandy*
1 stalk celery, chopped   *½ cup tomato sauce*
1 clove garlic, diced   *1 tablespoon cornstarch*
2 whole cloves   *Brandy*

Season the meat with 1 tablespoon salt and freshly ground pepper. Place it in a good-size bowl. Combine the vegetables, cloves, and herbs with the wine and brandy. Pour over the meat. Cover with foil and marinate in refrigerator about 5 hours. Turn occasionally. Remove meat, drain—reserving marinade—and pat dry with paper towels. Heat a little fat trimmed from the meat in a heavy skillet. Place meat in skillet and brown on all sides.

Have a large sheet of heavy duty foil ready on a shallow pan. Place the meat in the center. Pour off fat in skillet, then add the marinade, letting it simmer until reduced to about 1 cup. Pour this over the meat. Add ½ cup tomato sauce and the bones if used. Bring the foil up over the meat; seal airtight with double fold. Seal both ends. Place in a 300°F oven; cook 3½ hours. Test for tenderness. Remove meat to a serving platter. Place a strainer over a saucepan and strain juices from foil into saucepan. Skim off fat. Mix cornstarch with brandy and add. Simmer until slightly thickened. Add additional salt and pepper if desired.

Good to know: This is a fine dish for buffet serving. The meat may be sliced, bordered with small white onions and carrots. Pour a small amount of the sauce over the meat, and sprinkle with chopped parsley. Cover with foil and keep hot on an electric hot tray or in the oven.

Great go-with: Buttered noodles are excellent with this.

LAMB ROLL WITH VEGETABLES   *(8 to 10 servings)*

5 to 6 pound shoulder of lamb, boned	*½ cup water*
1 clove garlic, slivered	*New red potatoes*
1 envelope onion soup mix	*Carrots, scraped and quartered*
1 envelope cream of mushroom soup mix	*Medium-size white onions, peeled*

Have butcher bone and roll lamb and trim off excess fat. Arrange a large sheet of heavy duty foil in a shallow pan and place lamb in center. Insert garlic slivers in small pockets cut in the lamb. Combine soup mixes with water; spread over lamb.

Close the foil, overlapping long ends 3 inches on the top of the roast, closing opposite ends by folding up tightly. Place in 350°F oven and roast for 3 hours. Peel potatoes, leaving band of skin around center. Open foil and add vegetables 1¼ hours before lamb is finished. Or the vegetables may be placed in a foil package with salt, pepper and butter to taste, and baked separately during last 1¼ hours. To serve, open foil at one end of roast package and pour juices into a saucepan. Skim off excess fat. Thicken with flour and water or serve plain. Place foil package with roast in center of serving plate and fold back foil attractively. Border with the vegetables.

HAM: FLAVOR-BAKED IN FOIL

Arrange a large sheet of Heavy Duty Reynolds Wrap in a shallow roasting pan and place ham in center. Pour half the amount of one of the sauces on page 46 over ham. Bring foil up, covering ham loosely. Bake according to chart. Half an hour before baking is finished, open and turn back foil. Spoon out melted fat; remove skin, if any. Score ham in diamond pattern and stud with cloves. Pour remaining sauce over. Insert meat thermometer, if used. Continue baking with foil open, basting with sauce, until nicely browned and glazed. Skim fat from pan juices and serve juices with the ham.

HAM BAKING TIMETABLE (Oven Temperature 350°F)

Fully Cooked Hams	Weight	Approximate Total Time	Meat Thermometer Temperature
Whole, with bone	8-12 pounds	3 hours	130°F
Half, with bone	4-6 pounds	1½ hours	130°F
Whole, partially boned	7-11 pounds	3 hours	130°F
Half, partially boned	3½-5½ pounds	1½ hours	130°F
Whole, rolled, no bone	6-10 pounds	2½-2¾ hours	130°F
Half, rolled, no bone	3-5 pounds	1-1½ hours	130°F
Canned Hams	3-6 pounds	1 hour	130°F
	6-10 pounds	1½-1¾ hours	130°F
Cook-Before-Eating Hams Whole, with bone	8-12 pounds	3½-4 hours	160°F
Half, with bone	4-6 pounds	1¾-2 hours	160°F

FLAVOR SAUCES FOR FOIL-BAKED WHOLE HAM

Frozen Orange Juice Sauce: Combine 1 can frozen orange juice, 1 cup brown sugar, ½ cup A1 Sauce.

Cider or Pineapple: Combine 1 cup cider or pineapple juice with 1 cup brown sugar. Decorate ham with pineapple slices.

Apricot: Combine 1 cup apricot nectar with ½ cup honey or brown sugar. Spread over ham before baking and during glazing.

Sherry or Madeira: Pour 1 cup of the wine over ham before baking. To brown and glaze, sprinkle lightly with brown sugar and baste with additional cup of wine.

BAKED HAM, FRENCH STYLE

Remove the skin from the ham and trim away all excess fat. Rinse the ham to remove some of the saltiness; pat dry with paper towels. Place ham on foil in a shallow pan. For a whole ham, pour over 1 cup Madeira wine and sprinkle over ½ cup each sliced onion and carrots, a stalk of celery cut up, several parsley sprigs, 1 bay leaf, ½ teaspoon thyme. Close the foil loosely and bake according to above chart. Remove ham from oven, open and turn back the foil. Ladle juices into saucepan, skim off fat and discard vegetables. Simmer until reduced to 1 cup. Add 1 cup beef broth, 1 cup Madeira. Thicken with 1½ tablespoons cornstarch moistened with a little of the wine, and simmer for 5 minutes. While sauce is being made, score fat with a cookie cutter to make an attractive pattern. Sprinkle lightly with brown sugar and return to the oven to brown. When almost brown, baste with a spoonful of the Madeira sauce.

OLD VIRGINIA HAM

No holiday buffet, hunt breakfast or party would be complete without one of these wonderfully flavored hams, resplendent with glaze and decked out with a colorful border of spiced crab apples or other bright relish. Their flavor is pungent and very "ham-y"— you can't eat this ham in a sizable steak or main course serving. Rather, it is served thinly sliced between hot buttered biscuits, or a few thin slices are served with Crab Meat Imperial.

All country hams are cured by salting, long smoking, peppering, then aging. The real Smithfield has the heaviest cure. Soak these hams overnight or longer and scrub them to remove some of the pepper. (Lighter-cured country hams from some packers may not need soaking—directions on the wrapper will state.)

Place a large sheet of heavy duty foil on a shallow pan and place the ham in the center. Pour over 2 cups of a flavorful liquid—cider, dry wine and water (mixed half and half) or ginger ale. Bring foil up over ham and overlap 3 to 4 inches. Turn up ends to hold in liquid.

Place in a 300°F oven and bake for 4 to 5 hours, or until the small bone in the shank end is loose. Remove ham from foil; carefully pour out the liquid and fat and discard. Spread out the foil so that it lines the pan, trimming off excess. Remove the skin from the ham and return to the pan. (If fat is very thick, this may also be trimmed.)

A country ham may be decorated with fruit and glazed with any of the glazes (page 46), but generally it is just brushed with warm honey or sprinkled with light brown sugar and returned to the oven with the foil open. Raise the temperature to 375°F and bake with foil open just long enough to brown the ham lightly.

HAM BAKED WITH BEER GLAZE AND SAUCE *(10 servings)*

5-pound canned fully cooked ham	*1 teaspoon prepared mustard*
1 teaspoon packaged herbs (blend for use with salads)	*Green pepper rings*
	Pimento strips
	Parsley sprigs
½ cup brown sugar	*Cherry tomatoes*
¼ cup beer	

SAUCE

1 tablespoon brown sugar	*½ teaspoon prepared mustard*
1 teaspoon cornstarch	*¼ cup beer*
1 tablespoon vinegar	

Turn ham out on a board. Remove the gelatin to a saucepan. Slice the ham as thin as desired, then tie with a soft string so ham retains its original shape. Arrange a large sheet of heavy duty foil on a shallow pan and place ham in center of foil. Fold foil around sides of ham so it forms a tray. Combine herbs with sugar, beer and mustard. Spread over ham. Let stand about 2 hours at room temperature. Thirty minutes before serving, spoon juices collected in foil over ham and place the ham in a 400°F oven. Bake just long enough to brown top of ham lightly—20 to 30 minutes. Garnish with green pepper rings, pimento strips, parsley and cherry tomatoes.

BEER SAUCE: Heat the gelatin removed from ham. To ¾ cup of this liquid add brown sugar mixed with cornstarch, vinegar, prepared mustard. Cook, stirring constantly until thickened. Stir in ¼ cup beer. Sauce should have a delicate beer flavor.

UPSIDE-DOWN HAM LOAF (6 servings)

4 cups ground cooked
  ham (about 1 pound)
1 very small onion
2 cups herb-seasoned
  stuffing croutons
½ cup hot water

2 eggs, slightly beaten
¼ cup brown sugar
½ teaspoon ground
  cloves
4 pineapple slices

When you grind the ham, grind the onion right along with it. Soak croutons in hot water; add eggs, then ham, mix well. Line 8 by 3 inch loaf pan with foil. Sprinkle brown sugar, cloves over foil. Arrange pineapple slices on top. Press meat mixture into pan. Bake in 350°F oven for 1 hour. Turn out; peel off foil.

BRAISED SHOULDER OF VEAL (10 servings)

4 pounds veal shoulder in
  one piece, neatly rolled
3 tablespoons veal or
  beef fat OR salad oil
2 carrots, sliced
1 onion, sliced
2 stalks celery, sliced
½ cup tomato sauce
1 small clove garlic,
  crushed

1 teaspoon salt
⅛ teaspoon pepper
2 tablespoons cornstarch
2 tablespoons dry
  vermouth OR water
¼ cup sour cream
  (optional)

Heat fat or oil in a large skillet and brown meat on all sides. Place a large piece of heavy duty foil in a shallow roasting pan. Mix together carrots, onion and celery, put half of this mixture in center of foil. Place meat on vegetables and sprinkle remaining vegetables over it. Mix tomato sauce, garlic, salt and pepper and pour over meat. Seal the foil to make a tight package. Bake in a 300°F oven for 2½ to 3 hours. Open package, remove meat to serving platter, arrange vegetables around it. Ladle out the juice from bottom of package into a saucepan; skim off excess fat; add cornstarch mixed with vermouth or water and cook until thickened. Stir in sour cream, if used. Garnish with the vegetables.

VEAL CHOPS BONNE FEMME   *(4 to 6 servings)*

3 tablespoons veal fat OR salad oil
4 to 6 veal chops ¾ inch thick
2 tablespoons butter or margarine
1 onion, thinly sliced
¼ pound mushrooms, sliced

1 tablespoon flour
¼ cup dry white wine OR vermouth
¾ cup water
½ teaspoon salt
Pepper
Chopped parsley

Heat fat in skillet. Flour chops lightly, brown quickly on both sides. Line a shallow baking dish or pan with heavy duty foil and arrange the chops in it. Discard as much fat as possible from the skillet and add butter, onion, mushrooms. Brown the vegetables; arrange over and around chops. Stir the flour into fat in skillet, add wine, water, salt, pepper. Simmer until thickened and brown bits are dissolved, then pour over chops. Seal with a foil cover. Bake in a 300°F oven for 1 hour. Sprinkle with parsley.

Great go-with: This one calls for buttered noodles or creamy mashed potatoes.

HAMBURGER PIZZA   *(6 servings)*

1 can condensed tomato soup
1½ pounds ground beef
¼ cup fine dry bread crumbs
¼ cup minced onion
1 egg, slightly beaten

1 teaspoon salt
1 medium clove garlic, minced
⅛ teaspoon oregano, crushed
3 slices Mozzarella OR process cheese

Mix ¼ cup tomato soup with next seven ingredients in a large bowl. Place a square of heavy duty foil on a cookie sheet. On it, pat out the meat firmly into a 10-inch circle about ½ inch thick. Build a stand-up rim about 1 inch high around the edge of the circle. This makes a meat "crust" for your pizza. Be sure to make the meat rim high enough and firm enough so that it will prevent the meat juices and sauce from bubbling over. Turn up the edges of the foil to catch drippings. Spread remainder of the can of tomato soup over meat. Top with 3 slices of cheese and more oregano.

If desired, add anchovies or mushrooms. Bake at 450°F for 15 minutes or until done. Spoon off drippings in foil. Cut pie into wedges.

VERY BEST MEAT LOAF   *(8 servings)*

2 pounds ground beef	1 cup stale bread crumbs
¼ cup each chopped	2 eggs, lightly beaten
celery, parsley	½ cup evaporated milk
1 tablespoon grated	2 strips bacon
onion	1 6-ounce can mushrooms
1½ teaspoons salt	1 tablespoon instant
¼ teaspoon pepper	blending flour

Mix together beef, vegetables and seasonings. Add bread crumbs; combine eggs and milk, and add. Toss lightly with a fork until well mixed. Line loaf pan with Reynolds Wrap and place meat mixture in pan, shaping it into loaf form. Arrange bacon strips over top. Bake at 350°F for 1 hour.

To make gravy, tip pan and pour drippings into a saucepan. Skim off fat. Add mushrooms with liquid. Then stir in 1 tablespoon flour. Stir and cook until slightly thickened. Lift meat loaf to platter with foil. Slice and serve with gravy poured over.

Good to know: Store stale bread in the refrigerator. Grate it on a coarse grater to make crumbs.

With tomorrow in mind: You'll want to make twice the recipe of this meat loaf. Serve one loaf right away; cool, foil-wrap and refrigerate the other. For the second meal, take meat loaf from refrigerator and open foil. Combine 1 can condensed tomato soup and ¼ cup chili sauce. Spoon liberally over loaf. Close the foil up loosely and reheat in a 350°F oven for 30 minutes.

This is a wonderful way of cooking corned beef. The meat will be tender and juicy, deliciously flavored and wonderful either hot or cold.

CORNED BEEF IN FOIL

3 to 4 pounds corned beef	1 orange, sliced
¼ cup water	1 onion, sliced
2 tablespoons pickling	1 celery stalk with leaves
spice	1 carrot, sliced

Soak the corned beef in water to cover for ½ hour, or longer if deeply corned. Place a large sheet of heavy duty foil on a shallow pan. Remove corned beef from water and pat dry to remove any salt on surface. Place in center of foil and pour over it ¼ cup fresh water. Sprinkle with the spice and arrange orange slices and vegetables over and around the meat. Bring long ends of foil up over meat and seal with a tight double fold. Seal other ends, turning them up so liquid cannot run out. Bake in a 300°F oven for 4 hours. *Great go-withs:* Because this corned beef is so flavorful, a delicate creamed vegetable, such as cauliflower with mornay sauce, and a simple green salad make good accompaniments.

Good to know: Corned beef from the supermarket is usually less salty than that from a butcher who does his own corning and may have it in brine for several days. It will be deeper and more gray in color if corned for several days.

HOLIDAY HAM SLICES TUTTI FRUTTI *(6 servings)*

2 center ham steaks,
  1 inch thick
1 cup drained crushed
  pineapple
1 cup mixed chopped
  fruit (light raisins,
  maraschino cherries,
  cooked prunes)

1 cup brown sugar
1 cup pineapple chunks
¼ cup pecan halves
½ cup maraschino
  cherries
Mandarin orange
  sections

Place a sheet of heavy duty foil on a shallow pan and place one ham steak in center. Gash fat at 1-inch intervals, so ham will stay flat. Combine crushed pineapple with chopped fruit and half the brown sugar. Spread half this mixture over the steak; top with the second steak, sandwich-fashion. Wrap foil loosely. Bake in 400°F oven for 45 minutes. Remove from oven; roll back foil. Spoon out fat. Top with remaining fruit mixture, pineapple chunks, pecans, cherries, orange sections, remaining sugar. Return to oven 20 minutes to glaze, basting occasionally with liquid in foil.

HOT DOGGITIES *(4 to 5 servings)*

1 pound (8 to 10)
  frankfurters

½ cup ketchup
½ cup cornflake crumbs

Score surface of frankfurters lightly, spiraling from end to end. Insert wood skewers for extra eating fun. Roll each frankfurter in ketchup, then in cornflake crumbs. Place heavy duty foil on a shallow pan. Arrange frankfurters on foil; do not crowd. Bake in 350°F oven about 15 minutes. Serve with additional ketchup or mustard.

The Beautiful Birds

The Beautiful Birds

*The wisest poultry is foil-wrapped for quicker cooking,
more succulent results, never-before flavor*

Chickens and turkeys are among our most readily available and most delicious protein foods. Markets often have poultry on special sale, and at such times it is worth while to buy one or more turkeys, or a good supply of chickens, and store them in the freezer for future use.

Turkey and duck are usually purchased frozen; only occasionally can they be found fresh killed. Chicken, on the other hand, is plentiful the year round, and is usually sold fresh killed. All must have good care in the refrigerator and freezer to preserve their freshness, flavor, and nutritional value.

All frozen poultry: Get it home and into the freezer quickly if it is not to be cooked right away. If the package in which the birds are sold seems inadequate, give it a second wrap of Heavy Duty Reynolds Wrap.

Fresh turkey and chicken: If they are to be cooked within 2 or 3 days, wrap loosely in heavy duty foil and store on the refrigerator shelf. If to be kept longer, wrap in heavy duty foil and store in the freezer.

How to wrap turkey for freezing: Place bird (up to 15 pounds) lengthwise in center of a long sheet of 18-inch-wide heavy duty foil. For wrapping larger turkeys, join 2 widths of 14- or 18-inch-wide heavy duty foil with a tight double fold. Place the bird in the center and bring long ends of foil together up over top. Seal them with a tight crease, folding over and over until the fold rests on the bird. Mold the foil down over the turkey, pressing out the air, and seal ends by creasing and folding. Label bird with weight and date of purchase. Place in contact with sides or floor of freezer.

Thawing frozen turkeys: The best method is to remove bird from freezer several days ahead. Place on tray or shallow pan on the refrigerator shelf. Do not remove foil. Allow 1 day for a 6 to 8

In color picture: Roasted Turkey

pound bird, 2 to 3 days for birds up to 15 pounds, and 4 days for those over 15 pounds. How frequently the refrigerator is opened will affect the thawing time.

An alternate method is to leave the bird in foil and place under cold running water or in a deep pan of water and change the water frequently. Allow 2 to 8 hours for thawing.

A thawed or fresh ready-to-cook turkey can be kept on the refrigerator shelf at 38 to 40°F for 1 to 2 days. Loosen the foil on a frozen turkey when it has thawed. It is not advisable to refreeze.

How to wrap chickens for freezing: Chicken is least expensive when it has not been cut up. It may be left whole, or cut into halves, quarters or parts, depending on the way you are going to cook it. Arrange chicken in center of a large piece of heavy duty foil. If chicken has been cut up, arrange so bone ends are covered by fleshy parts of chicken—or they may be padded with small folds of foil. Bring two ends of foil together up over chicken and seal by creasing and folding the foil. Mold foil to chicken, pressing out air, and seal ends with tight fold. Label with contents and date.

Thawing frozen chicken: Don't attempt to broil or fry from the frozen state, as the center of the chicken is likely to be raw when the outside is done. You can begin to stew or fricassee chicken while it is frozen. However, it is always best to thaw on the refrigerator shelf before any kind of cooking, if possible. Chicken may be kept 1 to 2 days after thawing; if this is to be done, loosen foil wrap.

ROASTING TURKEY

Turkey is tasty, moist and delicious when roasted with the help of Reynolds Wrap—and this magic material can make turkey preparation much easier, too!

Oven ready turkeys require little beforehand preparation. You don't need to do an elaborate stuffing and trussing job; in fact, the turkey will be in the oven much faster if you don't stuff it. Bake the stuffing separately in a foil package or foil-lined casserole.

If you do stuff, use packaged stuffing and add your own touches for extra flavor goodness. If you make stuffing from scratch, use bread that has been stored in the refrigerator for several days ahead of time. Then grate it on a coarse grater. You'll find this an easy way to make crumbs.

PREPARATION FOR ROASTING

1. Start preparing turkey as soon as it is pliable enough to handle. Remove giblets, rinse and place in pan with onion, celery stalk, salt and pepper and water to cover. Simmer 1½ hours to make broth for use in gravy. Remove liver after five to ten minutes.

2. Rinse turkey with cold water, drain and pat dry. Rub cavities with salt, pepper and monosodium glutamate.

3. If turkey is to be roasted without stuffing, simply fold neck skin onto back and fasten with a skewer. Twist wings so tips rest on back. Place a few slices of onion and a celery stalk in body cavity; draw skin together and tie drumsticks to tail.

To stuff turkey, fill both neck and body cavities lightly with just enough stuffing for one dinner. Close as above. Use a small piece of foil over front opening to hold in stuffing if necessary. Bake extra stuffing in a foil package or foil-lined casserole during last hour of roasting.

ROASTING

Scientifically raised, modern turkeys are very young birds. They are heavily fleshed, but their meat is delicate and tender. Gentle, gradual roasting at low temperature with a foil tent placed over the bird after it has lightly browned produces a juicy, tender, picture-perfect bird.

1. Line a shallow roasting pan with just enough foil to cover the surface of the pan. Place a rack in the pan and the prepared turkey on the rack. Brush the bird with soft shortening.

2. Roast in a preheated 325°F oven, according to the following timetable:

TIMETABLE FOR TENT-ROASTED TURKEY (oven temperature 325°F)

Ready-to-cook Weight (pounds)	Internal Temperature	Approximate Roasting Time (hours)
6-8	185°F	3-3½
8-12	185°F	3½-4½
12-16	185°F	4½-5½
16-20	185°F	5½-6½
20-24	185°F	6½-7

Home and Garden Bulletin 110 U.S.D.A.

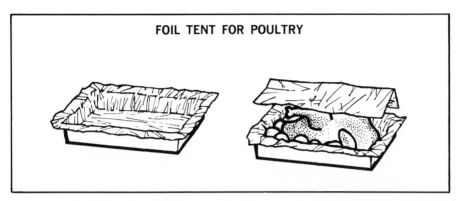

FOIL TENT FOR POULTRY

3. After the bird has lightly browned, cover with a loose tent of heavy duty foil. To make tent, tear a sheet of foil 5 to 10 inches longer than turkey. Crease lengthwise through center, then place over bird and crimp the foil a little at drumsticks and breast to anchor it. This will prevent over-browning and keep the bird moist and juicy without constant basting.

HIGH TEMPERATURE FOIL-WRAPPED
ROASTING METHOD

This method of completely foil-wrapping the turkey produces a juicy, very well-cooked bird, with some tendency for the skin and flesh to break. It saves time with very large birds.

Wrapping: Place prepared turkey on its back in middle of a large sheet of heavy duty foil. Turkeys up to 15 pounds may be placed lengthwise on a single sheet of 18-inch-wide foil. Join two widths of 14- or 18-inch foil together for larger birds.

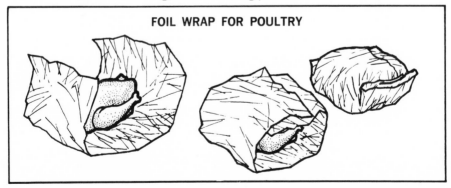

FOIL WRAP FOR POULTRY

Brush all over with soft shortening. Place small folds of foil over the ends of legs, tail, and wing tips to prevent puncturing. Bring long ends of foil up over the breast of the turkey and overlap 3 inches. Close open ends by folding the foil up 3 to 4 inches so drippings will not run into pan. Large turkeys may have as much as 3 pints of drippings. *Wrap loosely and do not seal airtight*—and do not use more foil than necessary to cover bird.

Roasting: Place wrapped turkey, breast up, in shallow pan and roast according to following chart:

TIMETABLE FOR FOIL-WRAPPED ROAST TURKEY
(oven temperature 425-450°F)

Ready to Cook Weight (pounds)	Internal Temperature	Approx. Total Cooking Time (hours)
7-9	185°F	2¼-2½
10-13	185°F	2¾-3
14-17	185°F	3½-4
18-21	185°F	4½-5
22-24	185°F	5½-6

Open foil 1 or 2 times during roasting to judge progress. When thigh joint and breast meat begin to soften, fold back foil completely to brown the turkey and crisp the skin. Insert meat thermometer at this time, if used.

HOW TO TELL WHEN TURKEY IS DONE: Birds differ greatly in size, shape, and degree of tenderness. Ovens vary in accuracy of temperature. Also, a turkey may be refrigerator cold or have warmed up to room temperature when it goes into the oven. For this reason a time chart is only a guide; it may be necessary to increase or decrease the cooking time.

A meat thermometer inserted in thickest part of the thigh should read 185°F. The drumstick and breast meat should feel soft when pressed with fingers (protect them with paper napkin). Drumsticks, thigh joint should move easily.

How to make wonderful gravy: Lift turkey onto a warm platter. Let it stand about 30 minutes so juices stop running and carving will be easier.

Pour drippings into pint or quart measuring cup. Skim off fat. Add broth made from giblets to make needed amount of gravy; pour into saucepan. If browned-on juices stick to foil pan liner, pour some of broth into pan, return to oven a few minutes to dissolve, then pour into saucepan. Bring to a boil. For each cup of broth, allow 1½ tablespoons flour. Mix flour with a small amount cool broth or water, then add to broth in saucepan. Stir and cook until consistency of heavy cream. Taste, add additional seasonings if needed, simmer a few minutes, and serve. For giblet gravy, add several tablespoons chopped giblets.

Roasting turkey breast-down: If you would like to try roasting a turkey breast-down, which some people believe makes the breast meat more moist and juicy, here is a way of doing it that will allow you to turn the bird breast-up during the latter part of the roasting time so it will look beautifully brown and crisp on top.

Plan to use the low temperature (325°F) tent method of roasting. Fold a long strip of Heavy Duty Reynolds Wrap in half, then in half 2 more times, to make a band 2 inches wide. It should also be long enough to go around the turkey with a little extra for good measure. Use two foil bands with turkeys 15 pounds and over.

Place a rack in the pan—the V-shaped rack which adjusts to accommodate various sizes of turkeys is best. Place the foil band on the rack; place prepared turkey breast-down, centered on the band. When turkey is about ⅔ done, remove from oven. Tug on one end of foil band and flip turkey over on wing side . . . another tug and onto its back. Foil band may remain under turkey. It will be long on the tugged end, so tear that off.

Return turkey to oven to finish roasting. When turkey is done, use the band to remove it to a warm platter. Just lift with both ends of the band. This is guaranteed to let you lift a heavy bird all by yourself without the use of a fork, potholders, or other aids!

Use a foil tent over turkey, both when it is breast-down and after turning. Place over the turkey when it has browned lightly. You can lift or remove the tent at will to observe browning.

Small turkeys, capons: Use foil tent method of roasting and low temperature time chart.

Half or quarter turkey: Tie leg to tail, wing to breast to make compact roast. If stuffing is used, mound on a piece of foil. Place on a rack in shallow pan; place turkey, cut side down, over stuffing. Brush with soft shortening and season. Roast in 325°F oven 2 to 2½ hours. Cover loosely with foil after turkey has browned lightly (30 to 45 minutes). Test for doneness as for whole turkey. Remove foil toward end of roasting time if not brown enough.

Turkey roll: Thaw turkey roll, if frozen. Place a sheet of heavy duty foil on a shallow pan; place turkey roll in center. Pour ½ cup white wine or vermouth over the roll, if desired. (Liquid is not necessary.) Brush with melted butter or margarine. Sprinkle with salt, pepper, herbs; surround with a few slices of onion. Close foil by overlapping it over the roll and turning up the ends. *Do not seal airtight.* Place in 350°F oven; roast 2 to 2½ hours. During last half hour, open foil and turn it back. Insert meat thermometer. Brush roll with melted butter or margarine; continue to cook until meat is nicely browned and thermometer registers 185°F. Gravy may be made from juices in foil in usual manner.

If turkey roll is precooked type, follow directions on the package. *Frozen stuffed turkey:* Frozen stuffed turkeys are now available during the holiday season in most areas. These should be roasted from the frozen state. Place a large sheet of heavy duty foil in a shallow pan. Place the turkey in the center and brush with melted butter or margarine. Close the foil by bringing the two long ends up over the bird and overlapping 3 inches. Turn up other ends, closing so juices will not run out. Place in a preheated 425° oven. Roast an 8 to 10 pound bird 3 to 3½ hours. Open foil during last 30 minutes to brown. Test for doneness (page 58). Prepare gravy as usual.

Storing leftover turkey and chicken: Remove stuffing and cool thoroughly. If leftovers are to be stored only for 1 or 2 days, just wrap in foil and store in the refrigerator. Wrap stuffing separately. If leftovers are to be stored longer, remove meat from bones, or cut the bird into compact portions; pad sharp bone ends with folds of foil and wrap in heavy duty foil. Seal edges with a tight double fold. Label (see page 183), and store in freezer. To serve, thaw frozen turkey; reheat in foil or serve cold.

Silver turkey platter: No platter large enough for the turkey? Just cover a large tray with Reynolds Wrap, securing it with tape. Garnish with lots of parsley.

If you must cook turkey ahead of time: Don't stuff it. Roast it by whichever method you prefer. When done, remove to a clean pan, cover very loosely with foil and let stand at room temperature for one hour, until some heat has left the bird. Refrigerate, allowing room for cold air to circulate around the bird. Prepare and cool gravy quickly, then refrigerate. Prepare stuffing ingredients . . . do not combine with liquid; refrigerate.

It doesn't improve turkey to reheat it but, if you wish to serve it that way, leave foil over bird and reheat it in a 350°F oven for 1 to 1½ hours. Combine stuffing with liquid and bake in a foil-lined casserole or package at this time. Serve the turkey with hot gravy.

CHICKENS ROASTED IN REYNOLDS WRAP

When whole broiler-fryers are on special sale, it is good practice to roast two or more at a time. Serve them all for dinner if your family is large, or serve one and refrigerate the other to serve cold or for the family to enjoy in sandwiches or as snacks.

Large roasting chickens weighing 4 or more pounds are also available in some markets. These are delicious roasted in foil and become a gourmet treat when savory flavoring ingredients are added to permeate the chicken while it roasts.

Roast small chickens together in one large foil package. Stuff or not as you wish. Large roasting chickens can be roasted together if two are being done at the same time.

ROAST YOUNG CHICKENS   *(4 to 8 servings)*

Purchase 2 whole broiler-fryers, each weighing 2 to 3 pounds. Rinse chickens and pat dry. Place necks and giblets in saucepan with an 8-ounce can of chicken broth, a small onion, a stalk of celery and ½ teaspoon salt. Simmer to make broth for gravy. If you wish, stuff chickens lightly. Fasten neck skin to backs with toothpicks, twist wing tips onto back and tie drumsticks to tail. Don't sew or lace opening. (This way the heat penetrates stuffing quickly, cooking it more thoroughly and making it lighter.)

Place a large piece of heavy duty foil on a shallow pan. Place chickens on foil. Brush with melted butter or margarine and season with salt and pepper. Bring long ends of foil up over birds and overlap. Turn up the remaining ends to hold in drippings. Do not seal.

Roast in 400°F oven 1¼ hours. Turn back foil during last 15 minutes; snip string holding drumsticks, baste chickens with drippings. Continue roasting until brown.

To make gravy: Pour drippings in foil into saucepan. Skim off excess fat. Add broth from giblets; thicken slightly, using 1½ tablespoons of flour mixed with a little cool broth for each cup of liquid; season to taste.

CHICKEN BAKED WITH MUSHROOMS AND HERBS
(4 to 6 servings)

1 4 to 6 pound roasting chicken
Mushroom Stuffing
2 tablespoons soft butter or margarine
¼ pound additional mushrooms

6 very small white onions, peeled
¼ cup vermouth OR white wine
1 teaspoon rosemary
Salt and pepper

Prepare chicken as for Roast Young Chickens. Make broth from giblets; stuff chicken lightly with Mushroom Stuffing. Place a large sheet of heavy duty foil on a shallow pan; arrange chicken in center. (If you don't mind turning it right side up halfway through roasting, place breast down for juicier breast meat.) Spread chicken with soft butter. Remove stems from mushrooms (stems may be added to stuffing) and arrange with onions around the chicken. Pour the vermouth or wine over. Sprinkle with rosemary, salt, pepper. Close foil by bringing two long ends up over chicken, overlapping slightly. Turn up other ends to hold in juices. Don't close airtight. Place in 400°F oven; roast a 4 to 5 pound chicken for 2¼ hours, a 5 to 6 pound chicken for 2¾ hours. Prepare gravy as for Roast Young Chickens.

MUSHROOM STUFFING

½ pound mushrooms
4 tablespoons butter or margarine
4 tablespoons minced onion
2 tablespoons celery with leaves, finely chopped

2 cups soft stale bread crumbs, OR
1 cup prepared stuffing
¼ to ½ teaspoon salt
Generous grating of pepper
½ to ⅔ cup chicken broth

Wipe mushrooms with a soft towel. Chop, then sauté them quickly in the butter. Remove, set to one side. Add onions, celery to same skillet; sauté until tender but not brown. Add bread crumbs or the prepared stuffing mix, and the salt and pepper. Stir over low heat to blend flavors. Remove from heat; add the mushrooms, moisten with the broth. Stuffing should just cling together.

ROTISSERIE CHICKEN

Modern ranges often have ovens equipped with rotisseries. And the rotisserie-broiler is a popular table-top appliance. Broiler-fryer chickens are ideal for this type of cooking. Buy whole chickens and prepare them as you would for roasting. If you stuff, openings must be securely closed, as stuffing may leak out when chicken revolves.

Run the spit through the chicken—the usual rotisserie will accommodate 2 to 3 broiler-fryers. Brush the chickens with melted butter or margarine—you may use additional seasonings as listed under broiled chicken (page 64)—and place the spit in the oven or rotisserie.

Line pan which will catch the drippings with foil. Let foil extend up the back of rotisserie or oven, to catch spatters. Turn on heat and "rotiss" the chickens about 1 hour or until tender and well browned. Baste frequently with additional butter or margarine and pan drippings.

INDOOR BARBECUED CHICKEN

Chicken may be barbecued either on a rotisserie or in a pan under low broiler heat. When using the rotisserie, brush with barbecue sauce (see page 170) as the chicken revolves during last 15 minutes. When using the broiler, follow directions for Savory Broiled Chicken and brush chicken with barbecue sauce about 15 minutes before chicken is done. Care must be taken, as barbecue sauces burn very easily.

Easiest, and a most appetizing, way of serving chicken is simply to broil it. Since it is low in fat, it may be placed directly on a sheet of Heavy Duty Reynolds Wrap for broiling.

Broiled chicken is wonderfully complemented by vegetables and fruits broiled at the same time.

SAVORY BROILED CHICKEN WITH CLING PEACHES

Purchase broiler-fryers split for broiling or in quarters. Place a large piece of heavy duty foil on shallow pan. Turn up foil 1 inch around edges to hold juices. Arrange chicken cut side up on foil. Brush with melted shortening, season with salt, pepper, and packaged mixed herbs. Place under broiler; broil slowly until brown. Turn skin side up and again brush with shortening and season. Continue broiling until almost brown. Place drained canned cling peach halves around chicken, brush them with shortening, spoon juices in foil over both chicken and fruit, and sprinkle with nutmeg. Continue broiling until chicken and peaches are nicely browned. It takes about 40 minutes to broil 1½ to 2 pound chickens. Pour juices in foil over chicken to serve.

Other broiled "chicken and . . ." combinations: Brush these foods with melted butter or margarine and season with salt and pepper. Arrange around chicken and broil last 10 minutes: firm tomatoes, cut in half . . . good-size mushroom caps . . . cold cooked white or sweet potatoes.

Vary the seasonings for broiled chicken. Add lemon juice, or a few drops of onion juice (made by scraping cut surface of onion) or a little curry powder to the melted butter. Seasoned salt may be used in place of regular salt.

CORN-CRISPED CHICKEN   *(4 servings)*

1 2½ to 3 pound broiler-   *1 cup corn flake crumbs*
  fryer, cut in serving   *1 teaspoon Ac'cent*
  pieces   *1 teaspoon salt*
½ cup evaporated milk   *¼ teaspoon pepper*

Dip chicken pieces in evaporated milk; roll in cornflake crumbs combined with Ac'cent, salt, pepper. Line shallow baking pan with heavy duty foil. Place chicken pieces, skin side up, in foil-lined pan; do not crowd. Bake in 350°F oven 1 hour, or until tender. If less crisp crust is desired, lay a piece of foil lightly over chicken. No need to turn pieces while baking.

COQ AU VIN   *(4 servings)*

1 3-pound broiler-fryer,   *2 tablespoons flour*
  cut in serving pieces   *1½ cups red or white*
½ cup diced salt pork or   *wine*
  bacon   *1 teaspoon salt*
4 tablespoons butter   *Generous grating of*
8 mushrooms, sliced   *pepper*
8 very small white onions   *1 bay leaf*
1 tablespoon diced onion   *1 teaspoon packaged*
1 small clove garlic,   *herbs for salads*
  minced   *Chopped parsley*

Use only the legs, second joints, wings, and breast pieces of the chicken, reserving the back and neck for soup. Rinse and dry the chicken. If diced salt pork is used (this gives the best flavor) parboil for 10 minutes and drain. Sauté the pork in a little of the butter until lightly brown. If bacon is used, simply brown it. Skim pork or bacon out of the pan and put to one side. Add remaining butter to skillet and, when hot, brown the chicken quickly and lightly. Place a large piece of heavy duty foil on a shallow pan; arrange the chicken on it and sprinkle the diced pork or bacon over it. Lightly brown the mushrooms, then the whole onions, in fat remaining in skillet. Arrange over the chicken. Pour off all but 2 tablespoons of fat from skillet and add the diced onion and garlic. Cook 2 minutes; blend in flour. Cook gently until flour just begins to brown. Add the wine, seasonings and bay leaf. Cook, stirring, until thickened, then pour over the chicken. Close the package by bringing longest ends of foil up over chicken, overlapping 2 inches. Turn up other ends so sauce does not leak out. Place in 300°F oven and bake 1¼ hours. Serve from package; remove bay leaf, sprinkle with chopped parsley.

Great go-withs: Pass crisp French bread and serve a green salad.

CHICKEN WITH TARRAGON CREAM BAKED IN FOIL
(4 servings)

4 small chicken breasts	*1 cup white wine* OR
¼ cup melted butter or	*vermouth*
margarine	*½ teaspoon tarragon,*
2 tablespoons flour	*fresh or dried*
½ teaspoon salt	*1 cup heavy cream*
¼ teaspoon white pepper	*3 egg yolks*
½ cup cognac OR *brandy*	

Remove small bones from chicken. Arrange cut side up on foil-lined shallow pan. Brush with melted butter, then sprinkle with half of flour, salt, and pepper. Place under broiler and broil until just tinged with brown—must not be well browned. Turn, again brush with butter and sprinkle with flour and seasonings. Broil the second side just a little. Pull out pan, pour brandy over chicken and light with a match—or just let brandy ignite from the broiler. When the flame goes out, remove pan from broiler and add the wine. Cover chicken with second piece of foil, sealing cover and liner tightly together. Set thermostat at 350°F and return chicken to the oven. Bake 45 to 50 minutes. Remove from oven, open one corner of foil and pour juices into a saucepan. There should be about 1 cup. If more, simmer to reduce. Skim off any fat. Add the tarragon. Beat the cream and egg yolks together with a fork and add to the chicken pan juice. Stir and cook gently until the sauce is slightly thickened.

To serve, transfer foil with chicken to warm serving platter or tray. Remove cover foil and turn up edges of foil under chicken to make a pretty border all around outside. (Snip foil with scissors into points or scallops, if desired.) Pour a little of the sauce over each chicken breast and serve the rest in an attractive sauce dish.
Great go-withs: Garnish with julienne carrots, tender green peas, tiny white onions, potato puffs, small orange cups filled with whole-cranberry sauce.

HOLIDAY ROAST GOOSE

Roast goose is a traditional holiday food and an excellent, less frequent choice for a festive menu. Goose has a lot of fat and, for the size of the bird, does not serve many. You will need a good carver, since, like duck, it is a bit unwieldy. However, it is possible to slice the breast meat and the short leg and thigh joints. An 8 to 9 pound goose will serve 5 to 6 people, a 10 to 12 pound bird about 7 or 8.

If frozen, thaw the goose, allowing two days on refrigerator shelf. Rinse, pat dry. Season inside and out with salt and pepper. Fill with Sausage and Apple Stuffing, or any other stuffing you enjoy. Tie the legs together with soft string, twist wing tips onto back. Line shallow roasting pan with heavy duty foil. Place a rack in the pan; place the goose on the rack. Roast in 350°F oven, allowing about 3½ hours for an 8 to 10 pound goose, 4 hours for 10 to 12 pound goose. Cover with a foil tent after it is brown.

To get rid of the fat, have ready a second foil-lined pan and remove goose from the oven and quickly transfer to the clean pan; or the fat can be spooned out or removed with a bulb baster.

One of the best parts of the goose is the crackling brown savory skin. To help the browning, brush the goose during the last hour of roasting with ¼ cup honey, combined with 2 tablespoons lemon juice, a little salt and pepper and ½ teaspoon each thyme and rosemary.

Test the goose for doneness as you would a chicken or turkey. When it is done, transfer to a warm platter and border with spiced crabapples or other tart spiced fruit. Make gravy as for turkey.

BUTTERY BREAD STUFFING

2 quarts stale bread
    crumbs
1 cup butter or
    margarine
½ cup chopped onion
1 cup chopped celery
2 teaspoons salt
Several gratings of
    pepper
2 teaspoons poultry
    seasoning
¾ cup hot chicken or
    turkey broth

The large oval loaves of unsliced Italian bread are excellent for making stuffing, since they become firm a day or two after purchase. If you use regular sliced bread, be sure it is several days old and let it stand outside the wrapper for a few hours to dry out. Crumb bread with the fingers or grate it on a coarse grater. Melt butter in a large kettle; sauté onions and celery until tender but not browned. Combine crumbs and seasonings, and add to the onions. Stir and heat for 5 minutes so all flavors are combined. Remove from heat; add the broth, moistening stuffing until it just begins to cling together. This will stuff a 15 pound turkey. For a 4 to 6 pound roasting chicken, use ¼ the above amounts.

Sausage Stuffing: Lightly brown ½ pound sausage meat, crumbling it as it browns. Add the sausage meat to the stuffing. Use 2 tablespoons drippings and ¼ cup butter to cook celery, onions.

Oyster Stuffing: Add 1 pint oysters out of shell. This is about 15 medium-size oysters. Slip the oysters through your fingers to make sure there is no shell. Strain the liquor. If the oysters are large, chop them. Use the oyster liquor as part of the liquid in moistening.

Fruit and Nut Stuffing: Add 1 cup tart apple (sautéed in 2 tablespoons of the butter), ½ cup raisins ½ cup chopped walnuts.

Chestnut Stuffing: Add 1 pound coarsely chopped, shelled, cooked chestnuts. Add sausage meat also, if desired, using amounts above.

How to Cook Chestnuts: Peeling chestnuts is a bit of a job. Do it ahead of time. Rinse the chestnuts; cut off a little strip of shell from one edge. Place them in a saucepan with cold water to cover; bring to a boil, boil 1 minute. Remove the pan from heat; pick out chestnuts a few at a time and peel off the shell. Peel off the inner brown skin also. If it doesn't come off, put chestnuts back in boiling water again for a few minutes. When all shells and skins are off, put the chestnuts in a saucepan with 1 cup broth and a little salt. Simmer until they can be pierced with a fork. Drain, cool slightly, then put on a board and chop coarsely.

The Wild Ones

The Wild Ones

Maybe you can't shoot your own game (or maybe you can!) but you can cook it to a turn, and better. Here's how

Cooking game with foil: For both city and country folk, game is now a fairly common food item. Markets carry pheasant and other game, particularly during fall and winter months, and the rock cornish hen is available everywhere.

Whether the hunter in your family or the market supplies you with game, it is usually stored in the freezer, since it is generally saved for special occasion serving. Heavy Duty Reynolds Wrap should be used for wrapping and packaging all game, since it provides the best protection against drying out and changes in flavor. It is also more convenient to use, since it molds to irregular shapes. Use the same method of wrapping as for poultry and meats. Don't keep game as long as domesticated poultry and meats, as the flavor is more intense and long storage does not improve it.

Be sure to thaw game before cooking, preferably on the refrigerator shelf without removing the foil wrapping. This will take two or more days for a large goose or venison roast. A quicker method is to place it under cold running water.

Freezing does not tenderize game and, since hunters can't select just prime young birds or animals, game is not always as tender and juicy as poultry and meat you buy in the market. However, the flavor is great—and, prepared with aluminum foil, game can be a zestful and unusual treat for family and guests.

ROCK CORNISH GAME HENS, FRUIT AND NUT STUFFING
Individual portion birds of about 1 pound are excellent for party service; larger birds are ideal for two people. Thaw the birds, rinse and dry, then season inside and out with salt and pepper. Stuff with this fruit stuffing: Sauté 1 tablespoon of minced onion in ¼ cup of butter or margarine until just tender. Add 1 cup soft stale bread crumbs, ¼ teaspoon salt and a little freshly ground

In color picture: Rock Cornish Game Hens with Fruit Stuffing pepper. Brown the crumbs lightly. Add ½ cup soft dark or golden raisins and ½ cup chopped pecans or walnuts. Toss together, adding just a little water or chicken broth to moisten. This will stuff two 1-pound birds. Fasten neck skin to back with toothpicks; twist wing tips onto back, tie legs to tail. Place a piece of heavy duty foil in a shallow roasting pan and arrange birds in center. Brush all over with melted butter or margarine.

Roast in a 425°F oven, basting with melted butter or margarine several times. Add 1 tablespoon of dry white or red wine to the butter and a sprinkling of herbs. When nicely browned—this will take about 30 minutes—close the foil by bringing edges together up over birds or, if several birds are in pan, cover with a second piece of foil. Do not seal airtight, since these tender little birds do not require much cooking. Continue roasting at the same temperature 30 to 40 minutes for individual portion birds and 50 minutes for larger birds. Look at them once during this period and, if juices have cooked away, pour on a little more melted butter and wine.

Birds are done when legs move easily. Remove trussing strings and serve with this sauce: Pour juices in the foil into a saucepan. Add a little more wine, a spoonful of currant jelly, salt and pepper, and simmer for 5 minutes.

Great go-withs: Arrange birds on carving board or platter. Spoon on a border of buttered rice with green pepper and pimento added for color. Garnish with spiced crabapples.

Good to know: Use a sheet of foil under carving board to protect table.

PHEASANT ROASTED IN FOIL

Pheasant is delicately flavored but, like most game, has a tendency to be dry.

Stuff each bird loosely with a few spoonfuls of wild rice stuffing and truss like Rock Cornish Game Hens. Place heavy duty foil in a roasting pan, add a cut-up stalk of celery with leaves, a slice or two of onion and a sliced carrot. Rub the pheasant all over with soft butter or margarine and place on the vegetables.

Roast in a 425°F oven for 40 minutes or until lightly browned, basting with melted butter to which a little white wine or chicken broth has been added. Close the foil up over birds or, if several pheasants are being roasted, cover with another piece of foil—just enough to hold in steam. Continue roasting another 40 minutes or until the leg joints move easily. If the pheasant is not tender at the end of 1¼ hours, reduce the heat to 300°F and continue cooking.

Lift pheasant to carving board or serving platter. Pour drippings into a saucepan, stir in flour and add chicken broth to make desired amount of gravy. Cook and stir until smooth. Carve the pheasant like a small chicken.

Great go-withs: Serve cranberry sauce, currant or other tart jelly. Parsley buttered potatoes, sauerkraut cooked with dry white wine and juniper berries, are traditional accompaniments.

ROAST WILD DUCK WITH CURRANT SAUCE

Not all wild ducks are good eating. The mallard is the most plentiful and best; teal and butterball are also good. Connoisseurs of wild duck usually want them roasted whole and generally have them dressed at a market where removing feathers and cleaning is handled by experts. They may be frozen; if not, they should be cooked within two days. As the flavor is quite gamey, don't stuff with any of the usual stuffings. Simply fill cavities with lemon wedges, slices of onion, celery tops and parsley sprigs. (These are for flavoring, not for eating.) Line a pan with foil, place a rack in the pan and arrange ducks on rack. Place strips of bacon or salt pork over ducks. Roast in a 450°F oven for about 40 minutes, basting with drippings and a little white wine several times. Remove bacon or salt pork as soon as it is brown. Remove duck to carving board and cover with foil to keep piping hot. Add a little brandy and about ¼ cup white wine for each duck to drippings in foil. Stir to dissolve browned-on juices, then pour into a saucepan. Skim off fat. Add 1 tablespoon currant jelly for each duck and simmer until jelly is melted and sauce concentrated. Slice breast and thigh meat of duck with a very sharp knife in thin slices. It should be rare. Pour sauce over.

Great go-withs: Wild rice, watercress and beautifully cooked brussels sprouts should go with this epicurean duck.

WILD DUCK, COUNTRY STYLE

There is little meat except on the breasts of wild duck. Also, it is hard to remove the feathers. Many people believe the best way to handle them is to cut out the breasts, remove the skin, and soak the breasts in a pan of water to which you have added 2 tablespoons of salt and 1 tablespoon of soda for each gallon. Or, if you wish to keep them whole, remove insides and skin them, then soak for about 8 hours. Salt and soda water help to remove the gamey taste. Be sure to cut away any shot or flesh marked by shot, as this will be strong. Rinse the ducks with fresh water, then dry. They may now be wrapped in foil and frozen, or cooked within a day or two.

Baked Duck Breasts: Arrange duck breasts in a foil-lined pan and sprinkle with salt, pepper, herbs, lemon juice, and top with strips of salt pork. Bake in a 375°F oven for 40 minutes, basting occasionally with a little boiling water or white wine and melted butter. Remove breasts to serving platter, pour drippings into a saucepan and remove all but a little of the fat. Stir in flour, add water or chicken broth and stir and cook until thickened. Add additional seasonings to taste.

Roast Whole Ducks: Fill cavities with sliced apples, onions, celery, carrots. Arrange in a foil-lined roasting pan. Place a slice of salt pork over each breast. Roast in a 375°F oven for 1 to 1½ hours, basting frequently with boiling water or white wine and melted butter. Discard stuffing. Cut ducks in half to serve them; make gravy as for duck breasts.

Great go-withs: Serve duck breasts or whole ducks with tart applesauce and wild or brown rice, hearty fall vegetables, such as turnips, cauliflower, or squash.

VENISON BRAISED IN WINE AND HERBS

4 pounds of venison	10 peppercorns
2 medium onions, sliced	6 juniper berries,
1 clove garlic, minced	crushed
1 carrot, sliced	1 teaspoon salt
Stalk of celery, with	½ cup salad oil
leaves	1 quart dry red or white
2 bay leaves	wine

Any cut of venison may be prepared in this manner. Prepare the meat for roasting, trimming off any tough parts. Tie with a soft string to make a compact roast. Combine the remaining ingredients in a large bowl for the marinade. The oil holds in the flavors of the marinade and keeps the meat from turning dark. (This marinade may be used for pheasant, rabbit and all game and helps to overcome gamey taste and to tenderize the meat.) Place venison in the marinade and cover the bowl with foil. Refrigerate for one to two days, turning the meat several times. Remove the meat and pat dry with paper towels. Heat 4 tablespoons of oil in a heavy skillet and brown the meat on all sides. Arrange a long piece of heavy duty foil in a roasting pan and place the meat on the foil. Add several fresh slices of onion, 1 cup of the marinade, and season with salt and freshly ground pepper. Seal the foil to make an air-tight package and roast in a 300°F oven about 3 hours. Transfer the venison to a serving platter or board and cover with foil to keep it warm. Pour juices in foil into a saucepan and add some of the marinade to make amount of gravy desired. Simmer it, then thicken with a mixture of flour and water. Strain and serve with the venison.

Great go-withs: Wild grape jelly and sauerkraut are delicious.

Good to know: Juniper berries are available at food markets.

ROAST VENISON

If the venison is young and tender, it may be roasted. Trim off parts that look tough. Venison has very little fat and tends to be dry. To overcome this, it needs to be larded. For a 4 or 5 pound roast, you will need ½ pound of fresh fat pork which has been cut into long ¼-inch strips. Pierce the venison at 2-inch intervals with a long thin knife and poke the fat into these holes with a wooden skewer. Rub the meat all over with a little garlic, herbs and pepper combined with salt. Line a roasting pan with foil and place the roast in it. Place it in a 450°F oven and roast for 30 minutes, turning the meat once. Insert a meat thermometer. Reduce the temperature to 350°F and roast until meat thermometer reaches 150° for rare or 160° medium rare, or allow 20 to 25 minutes per pound. When the meat is about half done, add 1 cup beef broth or dry red wine to the pan. Baste the meat with this liquid several times, adding a little more wine or broth if necessary. Cover meat loosely with a tent of foil. When meat is done, transfer to carving board or platter. Pour pan juices into a saucepan; skim off fat. Add additional broth or boiling water to make desired amount of gravy. Thicken with flour and water. Add a few tablespoons of dairy sour cream and salt and pepper to taste, to make a smooth, creamy gravy. Serve the meat sliced thin, with gravy spooned over.

Great go-withs: Potatoes with parsley butter, sweet and sour red cabbage or sauerkraut are traditional accompaniments.

ROAST WILD GOOSE

The wild goose feeds on grain and grasses, is less likely to be gamey than wild duck. It may be soaked in salt and soda water, but most people do not find this necessary. Simply rub the goose inside and out with lemon and fill the cavity with sliced apples, onions, celery and carrots. Twist wings under body. Place the goose on a rack in a foil-lined pan and cover breast with strips of salt pork. Roast in a 350°F oven, basting frequently with wine or chicken broth and drippings in pan. It will take about 3 hours for a 6 to 8 pound goose. Cover it with foil tent during the latter part of roasting time. To serve, discard stuffing, cut in quarters and then cut quarters in half. Prepare gravy and serve vegetables as for duck.

SAUERKRAUT, COOKED WITH APPLES AND SPICES
(4 servings)

Sauerkraut is a traditional accompaniment for game and most particularly for pheasant and venison.

Cover 1 pound of sauerkraut with cold water and bring it to a boil. Then drain it. Line a shallow baking dish with foil. Arrange the sauerkraut in the foil liner with 1 or 2 sliced tart apples, a sprinkling of crushed juniper berries, freshly ground pepper, thyme and bay leaf. Add white wine just to come to the surface of the sauerkraut. Cover loosely with foil and bake at 300°F for 2 hours. This may also be simmered on the surface of the range in a covered saucepan for 2 hours.

WILD RICE STUFFING

¾ cup (4 ounces) wild rice	*2 tablespoons chopped parsley*
3½ cups chicken broth	*Giblets, cooked*
1 small onion, chopped	*¼ teaspoon salt*
3 tablespoons chopped celery	*Grating of fresh pepper*
4 tablespoons butter	*¼ teaspoon poultry seasoning*

Wash rice through several waters; add to boiling chicken broth. Cook covered, stirring occasionally, for about 40 minutes or until all water is absorbed. Sauté onion, celery in the butter; add with chopped parsley, giblets and seasonings to the rice. Makes 3 cups of stuffing, enough for 2 pheasants, or 1 duck.

Sea
Bounty

Reynolds

Sea Bounty

Fish in a dish? Not any more! Here are dozens of ways to make it something much more special

Markets offer a tremendous variety of frozen fish products with all or most of the cooking done . . . and wonderful deveined shrimp, breaded shrimp, crab, and a great variety of frozen shellfish products. They make serving fish and shellfish simple. Often Reynolds Wrap can help with the few things that must be done to prepare these foods for the table.

Fish sticks: This popular fish product is fully cooked and needs only reheating. Form a pan of Heavy Duty Reynolds Wrap and arrange fish sticks in it. Heat, following package directions. Not even a pan is soiled!

Breaded fish squares, fillets: Form a pan of heavy duty foil and arrange the fish in it. Brush with melted butter or margarine and sprinkle with seasonings to taste. Bake or broil as package directs.

When time permits, you will want to create your own delectable fish dishes, to try wonderful French recipes. Either fresh or frozen fish may be used. Thaw frozen fish at least enough so fillets and steaks may be separated and handled before cooking. Select fresh fish and shellfish with care. It should be odor-free, firm, and bright of color.

Care of fish: Always store frozen fish in the freezer if it is to be held for longer than a few hours. It will thaw on the refrigerator shelf in 6 to 7 hours, and at room temperature in about 1 hour.

Wrap fresh fish in heavy duty foil, sealing tightly, and store in the coldest part of the refrigerator. It is best used the day it is purchased. But if fresh caught, it may be kept for 3 days. Wrap in foil and freeze if to be kept longer.

BROILING FISH

One of the easiest and most delicious ways of preparing fish is to broil it. Because most fish is low in fat, it does not have to be

In color picture: Broiled Fish

placed on the rack of the broiling pan as meat does. Instead, follow these simple directions:

Line the bottom of the broiler pan with heavy duty foil, or use a sheet of the foil on the broiler pan rack or on a cookie sheet, turning the edges up 1 inch all around to hold juices. (Don't use too large a piece of foil. Juices should be held close to fish so they do not dry out or burn. This way the fish stays nice and moist.)

Place butter or margarine on foil; place under broiler just long enough to melt. Remove; dip fish in this shortening, coating both sides. Sprinkle with lemon juice, seasonings; place under broiler flame or electric unit, allowing 2 to 4 inches between heat and fish. Broil until nicely browned.

Turn split whole fish, thick steaks and thick fillets. Thin fish does not need turning. Broil skin side first. Sprinkle with seasonings on second side, if turned. Broil second side until nicely brown. Fish is done when it can be easily flaked with a fork, but is still moist.

Serve fish right from foil, or transfer foil and fish to serving platter, crimping edges of foil attractively. Later use foil to hold bones and scraps.

Broiled fish is delicious served with the pan juices and lemon. Additional serving suggestions and sauces, page 91.

How long to broil fish: This depends to a considerable extent on the broiler. If the broiler works well, fish broils in a very short time. The great danger in cooking fish is overcooking. It is usually done as soon as it is brown. Thin fillets require only 6 to 7 minutes total broiling, thicker fillets and steaks about 6 minutes on a side. A whole 3-pound fish, split for broiling, will require about 10 to 12 minutes a side. Set the timer so you won't overbroil.

Turning fish during broiling: To turn a large steak or whole split fish without breaking it, use second piece of foil, the same size as the fish, right under the fish. When first side is brown, slip one or two broad spatulas under this foil; turn it with the fish. Peel it off, brush second side with shortening, sprinkle with seasonings; continue broiling.

BROILED SCALLOPS   (4 servings)

*1 pint or pound fresh or
    frozen scallops*
*½ cup melted butter or
    margarine*

Salt and pepper
Paprika
2 tablespoons flour

If the scallops are fresh, run them through your fingers to remove bits of shell. Spread out fresh or frozen scallops on paper towels, pat them dry. Line a shallow pan with foil and place butter and scallops in it and turn to coat both sides. Sprinkle with the seasonings and sift the flour lightly over them. Place under a hot broiler and broil small bay scallops not more than 8 to 9 minutes, sea scallops 10 to 12 minutes. Turn sea scallops once using a broad spatula or pancake turner. Serve with tartar sauce.

PAN FRIED OR SAUTEED FISH FILLETS

Almost any fish fillets or small whole fish are delectable if sautéed quickly and served with lemon or one of the accompaniments listed below. Fish cooks quickly, so don't overcook. For a crisp coating, the fish may be dipped in seasoned flour or cornmeal. But the most delicate fish does not need this treatment.

To avoid messy cleaning, line the skillet with heavy duty foil. Care must be taken not to puncture the foil with a fork or edge of spatula. A piece of foil arranged tent-fashion over the skillet during frying—it should not cover tightly—will catch spatters and keep the range clean.

Melt butter, margarine or shortening in the skillet; there should be enough to cover the bottom of the pan to a depth of ¼ inch. Heat it until very hot but not smoking, and place the fish in it. Brown quickly on one side, lift edge with spatula to test progress and use spatula to turn and brown second side. The fish is usually done as soon as it is brown. Test to see if it flakes. Drain on paper towels and transfer quickly to warm plate.

Fish is sweet, somewhat soft and delicately flavored. Accompaniments that contrast in flavor and texture help to make even the simplest fish dishes out of the ordinary. Try the accompaniments below; also the sauces listed on page 91.

BROILED OR SAUTÉED FISH FILLETS AMANDINE: Melt ½ cup butter in a small skillet, add ½ cup slivered almonds and sauté the almonds over low heat until they begin to turn a delicate golden color. Add 1 tablespoon lemon juice, 2 tablespoons dry white wine or vermouth, if desired, and a sprinkling of salt and pepper. Shake the pan over the heat for 2 minutes, then pour contents over the fish. This is enough for 1 pound of fillets or a 1-pound whole fish, such as trout or flounder.

BROILED OR SAUTÉED FISH FILLETS VERONIQUE: Use ¾ cups seedless grapes in place of the almonds and sauté just long enough to soften slightly.

BROILED OR SAUTEED FISH FILLETS, TOMATO AND HERB GARNISH: Use 1 cup cherry tomatoes, 2 tablespoons each chopped chives and parsley; 1 teaspoon chopped fresh basil and tarragon or a pinch each of the dried herbs. Sauté tomatoes, herbs very quickly in ¼ cup butter. Tomatoes should just begin to soften.

PLANKED FISH STEAKS DUCHESSE

Place a sheet of heavy duty aluminum foil on broiler pan rack and grease lightly. Turn up edges of foil one inch all around. Arrange on the foil thick steaks of any firm fresh or frozen fish or a whole fish, split. Brush fish with melted margarine; season with salt, pepper and lemon juice. Broil until nicely browned, then turn; again brush with melted shortening and season. Brown second side very lightly. Slip foil with fish onto a wooden plank which has been warmed while fish broiled. Surround the fish with cooked buttered carrots and peas. Use a pastry bag to pipe Duchesse Potatoes around outer edge, or spoon them on. With scissors, cut turned-up edges of foil attractively in scallops. Return to broiler to finish browning fish and lightly brown vegetables. Garnish with lemon cups filled with whole-berry cranberry sauce.

DUCHESSE POTATOES: Peel potatoes, cut in quarters, and boil in salted water. Drain thoroughly; shake over low heat to dry out. Put potatoes through ricer. For approximately 4 cups of potatoes, heat ½ cup milk with 4 tablespoons butter or margarine. Add to the potatoes, whipping with a whisk or electric beater. Add 1 small egg and continue beating until very fluffy. Season to taste with salt and freshly ground pepper.

SIMPLE POACHED FISH   (3 servings)

1 pound fish fillets, steak, or a thick piece
¼ cup dry white wine OR vermouth OR
2 tablespoons lemon juice plus 2 tablespoons water

¼ teaspoon salt
Generous grinding of pepper
4 tablespoons butter
2 tablespoons flour
Light cream (optional)
Chopped parsley

A deep skillet or saucepan will be needed for this poaching method. Fill it with about 1 inch of water. If you have a trivet, place it in the bottom. Bring water to gentle boil. Arrange the fish on a piece of heavy duty foil, cupping the foil around the fish. Add the wine or lemon juice and water, seasonings and 2 tablespoons butter. Place it in the saucepan. Cover the pan and cook gently for 10 to 15 minutes or until fish flakes with a fork. This is an excellent method of poaching fresh salmon or cod. When done, remove foil and fish. Tip the package and drain juices into a measuring cup. Discard the boiling water; in the same pan melt remaining 2 table-spoons butter, stir in flour. Cook gently for 2 minutes. Add the hot fish juices and additional wine and/or light cream to make 1 cup. Stir and cook until blended, smooth, and about the thickness of custard. Taste and correct seasonings.

Place foil with fish on a warm serving platter and turn back the foil. Pour the sauce over and sprinkle liberally with chopped parsley. Cod should be given an additional garnish of sliced or quartered hard-cooked eggs.

If you live near the water, you probably have whole fish to prepare. Stuff them or not as you prefer, but definitely let Reynolds Wrap bake them.

BAKED FISH WITH LEMON-HERB STUFFING

(8 to 10 servings)

3 to 4 pound whole fish	*1 tablespoon lemon juice*
Salt and pepper	*Lemon slices*
Lemon-Herb Stuffing	*Parsley*
½ cup melted butter or	
margarine	

Select any good-size, firm-fleshed fish. Bass, rockfish, pike, whitefish, salmon, red snapper, flounder and pompano are all good. The head and tail may be left on if you want to serve the fish in gourmet style, but it's usually easier to handle if they are removed. Scale and clean the fish and remove gills. Sprinkle it all over with salt and pepper, and fill the cavity with Lemon-Herb Stuffing, or use stuffing mix prepared according to package directions. Close opening by binding soft string around the fish. Arrange heavy duty foil on a shallow baking pan; brush with melted butter or margarine. Place fish on the foil. Add lemon juice to remaining melted shortening and pour over fish. Bring foil up around fish, folding it to form a boat that will help keep fish in shape. Bake in 400°F oven allowing 12 minutes per pound. Baste once or twice with juices that form in the foil. To serve: remove string, place foil and fish on serving platter; or serve right from pan. If sauce is needed, melt an additional ½ cup butter, add ¼ teaspoon salt, a grating of pepper, and 1 tablespoon lemon juice. Pour over each serving. Garnish with lemon slices and parsley.

LEMON-HERB STUFFING FOR FISH

3 cups coarse crumbs from white crackers
½ cup butter or margarine
¼ cup chopped onion
½ cup chopped celery with leaves
Grated rind of 1 lemon

1 tablespoon lemon juice
¼ teaspoon thyme
½ cup chopped parsley
½ teaspoon salt
Generous grinding of pepper

Roll and crush the crackers with a rolling pin. Melt butter in a skillet; add onion and celery, and sauté until tender but not brown. Add cracker crumbs, other ingredients; toss with fork over low heat until combined. Add a very little boiling water, so that mixture just begins to cling together. Taste; add salt if needed. Will stuff a 4 pound fish.

BAKED STUFFED FISH WITH SAVORY TOMATO SAUCE
(8 to 10 servings)

3 to 4 pound whole fish
Salt and pepper
1 cup packaged stuffing, prepared
Melted bacon drippings
1 small onion, sliced
½ small garlic clove
2 tablespoons butter

1 1-pound can tomatoes, drained
2 teaspoons each: minced fresh basil, parsley
2 to 3 slices bacon or salt pork

Sprinkle the fish inside and out with salt and pepper, and stuff. Bind with soft string. Arrange foil on a shallow pan and brush with melted bacon drippings or other fat. Place the fish on foil and fold the foil up around the fish to form a boat. Leave a little space for sauce. Sauté the onion and garlic in butter for 2 minutes; add the tomatoes (breaking them up), basil and parsley. Pour this over the fish. Place bacon slices over top of fish. Bake in a 400°F oven, allowing 15 minutes per pound. Baste once or twice with sauce in foil. Remove string and transfer foil with fish to serving platter.

WHOLE SALMON, BAKED WITH WINE AND HERBS

A 7 to 10 pound salmon will fit the average oven. For a special occasion leave the head on; trim the tail to an attractive length. Rinse the fish, pat dry, sprinkle with salt and pepper. Heat 2 cups dry white wine such as Chablis or 8 tablespoons lemon juice plus 1½ cups water. Add ¼ teaspoon each: dried thyme, basil, tarragon and rosemary. If fresh herbs are available, use 1 or 2 sprigs of each herb. Add also 4 tablespoons minced onion or shallots, a few celery leaves, a small slice of lemon rind and 4 peppercorns. Let this steep (almost but not quite boil) for 20 minutes. Place a sheet of heavy duty foil a little longer than the fish on a very shallow baking pan. (If the pan isn't long enough, use a second piece of foil, folding it so that it is longer and about as wide as the fish. Place this underneath the foil that will be used to wrap the fish and let it extend beyond edge of pan. This forms a firm foundation to hold fish.) Brush foil where fish will rest with a little butter or margarine. Place the fish on the foil and pour the warm wine mixture over. Bring foil up over fish, overlapping on the top about 3 inches. Close and turn up the ends. Place in a preheated 300°F oven; bake for 12 to 15 minutes per pound. An 8-pound fish will take approximately 1 hour.

The wine and herbs flavor the fish with an elusive and delicate taste Open the foil when the baking time is about up. Test for doneness by inserting a fork in the side. If the flesh flakes easily, it is done. Close foil and continue baking, if not done.

While fish is baking, start the sauce. Mince 2 shallots or 1 small onion and sauté with ½ cup of butter until transparent. Add 6 tablespoons flour and cook gently, stirring, for 3 minutes. Do not allow to brown. Let stand until fish is done.

Remove fish from oven. Form a pouring spout in foil at one end and carefully tip pan with fish letting liquid run out into a 1-quart measuring cup. Add ½ cup wine and enough boiling water to make 4 cups liquid. Add to butter mixture in saucepan. Cook mixture, stirring, until thick and smooth. Add ½ cup cream, and additional salt and pepper to taste. Just before serving, add the lightly beaten yolks of 1 or 2 eggs and beat sauce over low heat with a whisk until light. Do not boil. Strain into a sauceboat.

Leave salmon in foil to transfer to a serving platter. If a platter large enough to hold the fish is lacking, a piece of plywood covered with foil can be used.

The baking foil may be folded back and rolled down to make an attractive container. Remove the skin from the fish; it lifts off easily to expose tender moist flesh of an exquisite pink tint. Remove seasoning herbs. Surround the fish with tender chicory, fresh basil, lemon wedges and even small flowers of the season. Serve the sauce separately. An 8-pound salmon will serve 12 to 14 people generously. What is left over will be delicious served cold with mayonnaise.

Salmon Baked in Foil: A piece of salmon can be baked in exactly the same manner as whole salmon. For 3 to 4 pounds, use half the wine-herb mixture and make half the amount of sauce. Allow 15 minutes per pound in a 325°F oven.

QUICK-AND-EASY BAKED FILLETS OR STEAKS

Either fresh or frozen fish fillets may be prepared by this method. Thaw frozen fish until it can be separated. Cut fish into serving-size portions. Place a piece of heavy duty foil just a little larger than the fish on a shallow pan; turn up edges all around. Place butter or margarine on foil and put in the oven to melt. Remove pan; dip fish in the butter, coating both sides. Arrange the fish close together on the foil. Sprinkle with salt, pepper, paprika, lemon juice. Bake in a 425°F oven 15 to 20 minutes or until fish can be flaked with a fork. If desired, sprinkle with crumbs and baste with the juices in the foil during the last 5 minutes of baking. Serve with pan juices and tartar sauce.

CORN-CRISPED FISH   (3 servings)

*1 pound fish fillets or
  steak, cut in serving
  pieces
½ cup evaporated milk
1 cup cornflake crumbs
½ teaspoon salt*

*¼ teaspoon pepper
Generous sprinkling of
  paprika
¼ cup melted butter or
  margarine*

Dip fish in evaporated milk; roll in crumbs to which seasonings have been added. Place a sheet of foil on a shallow pan and turn up the edges all around. Brush with a little melted shortening. Arrange fish on foil, pour remaining butter over it and bake in a 375°F oven for about 20 minutes. Serve with any fish sauce.

FISH STEAKS BAKED WITH MUSHROOMS *(6 servings)*

*2 pounds fish steaks
    about ¾ inch thick
    (fresh or frozen)*
*1 tablespoon butter or
    margarine*
*2 small onions, sliced
    thin*
*1 6-ounce can broiled
    sliced mushrooms
    (drained)* OR

*½ pound fresh
    mushrooms, sliced*
¾ teaspoon salt
Freshly ground pepper
*½ teaspoon mixed herbs
    for seasoning fish*
*½ cup cream or
    evaporated milk*

If fish is frozen, thaw it. Place fish steaks in the center of a large piece of heavy duty foil. Melt butter in a small skillet; separate onion slices into rings and add, with mushrooms. Cook onions and mushrooms lightly over low heat about 3 minutes; arrange around fish. Sprinkle with salt, pepper, mixed herbs. Rinse the skillet with the cream and pour over fish. Bring the foil up over the fish and seal to form tight package. Place in shallow pan and bake in 325°F oven 1 hour. When done, slip package onto a hot platter. Open at table, turning back foil.

CLASSIC FRENCH FISH DISHES, SIMPLIFIED

The French have a way with fish that produces a dish incomparable in flavor and beautiful to look at.

First they poach (simmer) the fish in a flavorful liquid. Then they prepare a sauce from the poaching liquid and pour it over the fish. You can stop here and have a delicious, moist and flavorful fish dish to serve the family. But for further embellishment, shellfish, mushrooms or other flavorful vegetables may be added. And as a final touch, the beautifully arranged dish is placed under the broiler to give it a final glow of appetizing perfection.

A serious student of French cuisine, in preparing one of the classic fish dishes, would go through many steps and use a variety of utensils. Today, even noted French chefs are using aluminum foil to simplify the preparation of these formerly elaborate fish dishes.

On page 81 we give a method for poaching fish in a skillet or saucepan. The following method is for poaching fish in the oven. Both methods are excellent, but when large amounts of fish are to be prepared oven poaching is easier, and the delicate flavor of the fish is retained to an even greater degree.

FISH POACHED IN WHITE WINE   *(3 to 6 servings)*

1 to 1½ pounds fish	*Salt and pepper*
fillets or steaks	*3 tablespoons butter*
1 small onion, minced	*3 tablespoons flour*
2 or 3 parsley sprigs	*½ cup light or heavy*
1 tablespoon butter or	*cream*
margarine	*¼ cup grated Swiss or*
¾ cup white wine, OR	*Parmesan cheese*
¼ cup lemon juice plus	
½ cup water	

Place a large sheet of Heavy Duty Reynolds Wrap on a shallow pan. Sprinkle half the onion in the center and arrange the fish on it, overlapping thin fillets. Very thin fillets may be rolled up, jelly-roll-fashion, and secured with toothpicks, or they may be folded in half. Sprinkle remaining onion and parsley sprigs over the fish. Dot with butter. Pour the wine or lemon-and-water over. Sprinkle with salt and pepper.

Bring the long ends of the foil up over the fish and seal with a tight double fold. Seal other ends by folding and turning up to hold juices.

Bake in a 375°F oven for 12 minutes. Open one corner of the package and gently pour out the liquid into a measuring cup. There should be a little more than 1 cup. Place package with fish on a heatproof platter or serving dish. Remove parsley.

In a small saucepan, melt 3 tablespoons butter and blend in 3 tablespoons flour. Cook, stirring, for 3 minutes, then add the hot fish liquid and continue stirring and cooking until smooth. Add the cream, using just enough to make a creamy sauce of not quite medium consistency. Taste and add additional seasonings, and a few drops of lemon juice, if needed.

Open and turn back the foil holding the fish. Crimp it to form a pretty border. Pour hot sauce over. Sprinkle with cheese; brown lightly under the broiler. This dish may be prepared ahead except for the final browning. Reheat in the oven for a few minutes, then brown under the broiler.

Good to know: This recipe is more truly French if you omit the grated cheese, and fold 2 tablespoons whipped heavy cream into the sauce just before pouring it over the fish. Brown under the broiler.

SOLE BONNE FEMME: Use fillets of a delicate white fish and start preparing as in basic recipe. Just before seasoning the fish, add ½ pound mushrooms prepared as follows: Slice mushrooms, sauté in 3 tablespoons butter for 3 minutes, tossing and heating them without browning. Spread over the fillets. Use additional salt and pepper and continue as in basic recipe.

SOLE BONNE FEMME WITH POTATO BORDER: Have ready 2 cups of freshly mashed potatoes which have been whipped with plenty of butter, milk and seasonings. Just before pouring on the sauce, arrange the potatoes around the fish. They may be forced through a pastry bag or spooned around. Pour on sauce and brown.

FISH FILLETS WITH JULIENNE VEGETABLES: Start preparing fish fillets as in basic recipe. While fish is baking, prepare vegetables cut in ¼-inch x 2½-inch matchstick lengths: 1 cup carrots, 1 cup celery, ½ cup yellow onion. Simmer the vegetables in boiling salted water until barely tender. Drain. When fillets are baked and foil turned back, arrange vegetables to form border. Pour sauce over and continue as in basic recipe.

FISH FILLETS WITH SHRIMP SAUCE: Prepare fish fillets as in basic recipe. Just before seasoning fish, add ½ pound small, uncooked shrimp—shelled, and deveined. The shrimp may be arranged as a border around the fish. Use a little additional seasoning for the shrimp. Continue as in basic recipe.

FISH FILLETS WITH SHRIMP SAUCE (quick method): Prepare fish fillets as in basic recipe. After baking, open corner of foil and pour juices into a saucepan. Simmer to reduce the quantity to about ¼ cup. Add 1 can partially defrosted frozen shrimp bisque. Cook, stirring, until a smooth creamy sauce is formed, adding a little cream to give the right consistency. Taste and add additional seasonings if needed. Turn back foil, pour sauce over fillets, sprinkle with Parmesan cheese and brown.

Many people like the idea of preparing fish in individual packets —a complete entrée to be served at the table in foil. Each person opens his own package and savors the wonderful aroma that bursts forth. This is "en papillote" cooking made famous by Antoine's, a well-known New Orleans restaurant.

FISH FILLETS IN A PACKAGE   *(3 servings)*

1 pound fish fillets, fresh	*1 or 2 very thinly sliced*
or frozen	*carrots*
1 small onion, sliced or	*Salt and pepper*
chopped	*Paprika*
3 tablespoons butter	

Thaw fillets, if frozen, until they can be easily cut. Divide fish into 3 portions. Prepare 3 squares of heavy duty foil about 14 inches square. Arrange fish in center of each. Add remaining ingredients, dividing equally; sprinkle with the seasonings. Bring foil up over fish; seal edges together with a double fold. Seal other ends in the same way, turning them up so that the juices will not run out. Place packages in a shallow pan and bake in a 400°F oven for 25 minutes.

Another way: To each portion add either 3 tablespoons undiluted condensed cream of celery or mushroom soup, or 3 tablespoons tomato sauce.

SAVORY BUTTERED SHRIMP   *(4 servings)*

1½ pounds medium-size	*Herb seasonings, such as*
shrimp in shell (21	*basil and rosemary*
to 25 per pound)	*½ teaspoon salt*
1 cup butter or	*¼ teaspoon freshly*
margarine, melted	*ground pepper*
1 small clove garlic,	*Tabasco sauce*
finely minced	
2 tablespoons lemon	
juice or white wine	

If frozen shelled deveined shrimp are used, thaw, do not boil. Fresh shrimp should be rinsed, then boiled in salted water to cover for 1 minute. Rinse again with cold water, then remove shells and dark vein; 1 pound in shell equals ½ pound shelled shrimp.

Form a pan from 2 thicknesses of heavy duty foil as follows: tear a sheet of heavy duty foil 14 x 18 inches; fold double, turn up edges all around to make a pan about 7 x 12 inches. Place on a shallow pan or cookie sheet for support. Put in the shrimp. To melted butter, add garlic, lemon juice or wine, herb seasonings and all other seasonings. Pour half over shrimp, coating well.

Place under the broiler 3 inches or more from the heat, and broil the shrimp lightly. Turn shrimp as soon as they become tinged a very light brown; spoon over more sauce and continue broiling— about 5 minutes for small shrimp, 8 minutes for larger. Baste with sauce several times. Shrimp should not brown deeply, but take on a lovely golden pink color.

To serve, slide the foil pan with shrimp onto a tray, spear shrimp with toothpicks and have ready crisp French bread to dunk in the wonderful sauce.

Good to know: This is a delicious appetizer to serve before dinner (8 servings) or it will make a feast for 4 people.

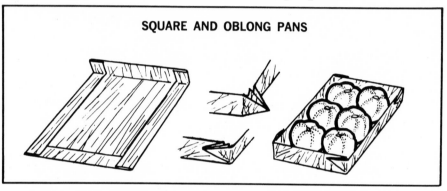

SQUARE AND OBLONG PANS

DEVILED CRAB IN FOIL CRAB SHELLS   *(6 servings)*

1 pound crabmeat
½ cup butter or
  margarine
½ cup chopped celery
1 small green pepper,
  seeded and finely
  minced
¼ cup finely minced
  onion
4 tablespoons finely
  chopped parsley
1½ cups soft, stale
  bread crumbs
1 teaspoon salt
¾ teaspoon dry mustard
Few drops Tabasco
¼ cup light cream

Pick over crabmeat, removing all shell and membrane. Melt butter in a good-size skillet; add celery, green pepper and onion. Sauté until barely tender but not brown. Add all remaining ingredients and the crabmeat, tossing lightly with a fork to blend. Fill individual foil crab shells or a foil-lined shallow casserole dish. Bake in a 350°F oven long enough to brown lightly—about 15 minutes.

FOIL CRAB SHELLS: Fold and cut heavy duty foil to make double-thick pieces about 6 x 4 inches. Form shells by placing a standard

90

8-ounce water glass or other medium-size glass on the foil pieces. Turn the corners of the foil at both ends toward the center and mold the center part of the foil up around the glass firmly. Twist each end to form a point. This is easy to do, forms attractive shells each holding about ⅔ cup. Place them on a shallow pan to fill and bake.

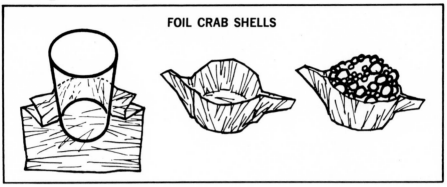

FOIL CRAB SHELLS

TARTAR SAUCE

1 cup mayonnaise
2 tablespoons lemon juice
2 tablespoons minced old fashioned dill pickle
1 tablespoon capers
2 teaspoons minced onion
2 teaspoons each: fresh tarragon, rosemary, thyme OR

¼ teaspoon each of the dried herbs
2 tablespoons chopped parsley
¼ cup dairy sour cream
¼ teaspoon salt
Generous grinding of pepper

Fold all ingredients into the mayonnaise.

MAÎTRE D'HÔTEL BUTTER

This is just butter, lemon juice and chopped parsley, but it's delicious on fish that is relatively fat-free. It may be prepared ahead, refrigerated or frozen, wrapped in foil. Cream ½ cup butter, adding 1 tablespoon lemon juice, drop by drop. Continue creaming, adding 2 tablespoons parsley. Enough for 1½ to 2 pounds of fish.

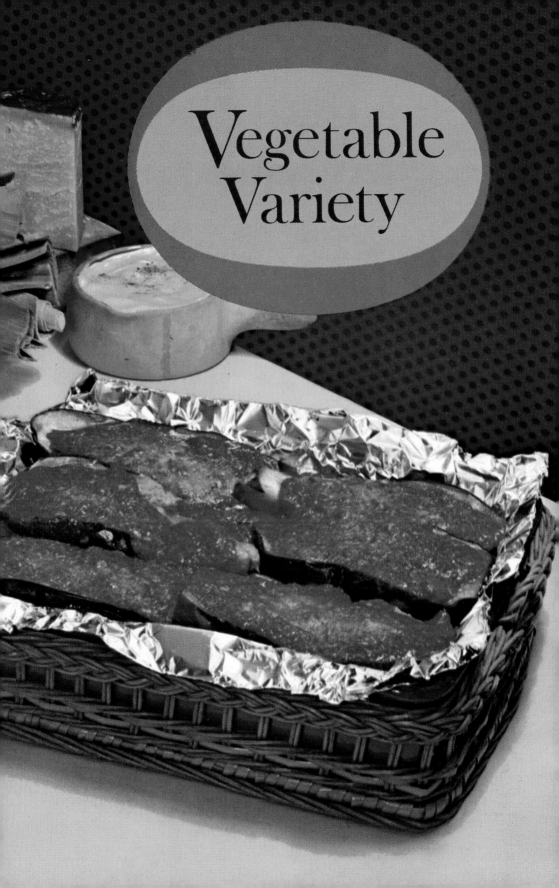

Vegetable
Variety

Vegetable Variety

Even children will eat them, and ask for more,
when they're fixed in these new ways

Both fresh and frozen vegetables are delightfully flavored, tender, and sweet when baked tightly sealed in a package of Heavy Duty Reynolds Wrap. Very little water is used, and the vitamins and minerals are not lost. The flavor and color are beautifully retained. This is not a fast method of cooking vegetables, but if the oven is in use for other foods, it is convenient and easy to cook them this way. The best oven temperatures are given for each vegetable, but other temperatures may be used by slightly shortening or lengthening the cooking time.

FROZEN VEGETABLES IN FOIL

Vegetable	Preparation	Time at 375°F
Asparagus, cut or whole	Add butter or margarine, salt, pepper, herbs, 2 tablespoons water	50 minutes
Cut corn, any style	"	50 "
Green beans, cut	"	50 "
Green beans, French style	"	45 "
Lima beans, small	"	50 "
Lima beans, large	"	60 "
Peas	"	35 "
Peas and carrots	"	40 "
Squash	Add all ingredients except water	35 "
Succotash	"	45 "
Wax beans	Add all ingredients	45 "

In color picture: Eggplant Parmigiana, Asparagus with Creamy Lemon Sauce

Remove frozen vegetables from freezer and open package a few minutes ahead, so the frozen block can be broken apart and vegetables separated. Place on a good-size square of heavy duty foil. Add 1 or 2 tablespoons water, butter or margarine, salt, pepper, and other seasonings as desired. Try adding chopped chives, parsley to frozen peas; tomato sauce, a slice of onion, and diced green pepper to corn; or combine two vegetables in one package. Bring foil up over vegetables and seal edges to form an airtight package. Place on a shallow pan and bake in oven according to the chart.

BUTTERED VEGETABLES IN FOIL CUPS

Tender carrots	*Salt and pepper*
Cauliflower	*Butter*
String beans	

Prepare vegetables for cooking by dicing carrots, separating cauliflower in flowerets, and cutting tender string beans into small snips. Prepare deep foil cups by molding heavy duty foil over water glass or other mold of proper size. Place a serving of vegetable in each foil cup. Stand cups in saucepan or deep skillet in 1 inch of boiling water. Add salt, pepper, 1 teaspoon butter to each vegetable. Do not close cups at top. Cover saucepan and cook 20 minutes for the vegetable combination above, or usual cooking time for others. Serve with delicious natural juices that form in each cup. Usually a saucepan will hold at least 3 servings of vegetables, each in a separate cup.

FOIL CUPS FOR VEGETABLES

ASPARAGUS WITH CREAMY LEMON SAUCE *(6 servings)*

Trim off tough ends of 2 pounds of asparagus and scrape off hulls that frequently hold sand. Use a potato peeler and peel off skin from lower stem ends—this makes the asparagus more tender and very handsome. Rinse and soak in cold water until sand-free. Gather stalks together and place on a long, 3-inch-wide strip of heavy duty foil. Use ends of foil to lower asparagus into boiling salted water and cook until tender, 10 to 12 minutes. A covered, deep skillet makes a fine asparagus cooker. Use ends of foil to lift asparagus from water. Drain on paper towels. Arrange on warm serving plates or platter.

CREAMY LEMON SAUCE

2 tablespoons butter or margarine
2 tablespoons flour
¼ cup fresh or frozen lemon juice
1 cup boiling water (from asparagus)

¼ teaspoon salt
Dash of Tabasco
½ cup dairy sour cream
1 tablespoon butter, melted

Melt butter or margarine in saucepan. Stir in flour and cook 2 minutes. Add lemon juice and water. Stir and cook until smooth and thickened. Simmer 5 minutes; add salt and Tabasco. Just before serving, add cream and melted butter. Serve over asparagus.

FRESH VEGETABLES IN FOIL

Choose tender young vegetables. In general, cut so they will cook quickly. Place packages on shallow pan; bake according to recipe.

FRESH PEAS IN FOIL

Shell 2 pounds fresh peas and place in center of square of heavy duty foil. Add 2 tablespoons butter, 2 tablespoons water, salt and pepper. To vary the flavor, add chopped fresh mint, slivered scallions, nutmeg, or thinly sliced mushrooms. Bring foil up over peas; seal edges to make tight package. Bake in 350°F oven 35 minutes.

FRESH ASPARAGUS

Trim off tough ends of 1 pound of asparagus; remove hulls and soak in water to remove sand. "French" the asparagus by cutting diagonally in ½-inch lengths. Place asparagus in center of large piece of heavy duty foil. Add 2 tablespoons butter or margarine, salt, pepper, 1 tablespoon lemon juice. Bring foil up over asparagus and seal to make a tight package. Bake in 350°F oven 40 minutes.

BAKED ONIONS *(6 servings)*

Peel 6 medium-size onions and prick through with a fork several times. Place in center of square of heavy duty foil. Drizzle 2 table-spoons honey over onions; add 2 tablespoons butter or margarine, salt and pepper. Bring foil up over onions, seal to make tight pack-age. Bake in 350°F oven 1½ hours. Small white onions given this treatment are also delicious, and so are large Bermuda onions. Bake small onions 1 hour; Bermuda onions 1¾ hours.

Good to know: Seasonings may be varied by adding 2 tablespoons lemon juice, tomato juice, or 2 tablespoons water in which ½ bouil-lon cube has been dissolved.

BAKED WHOLE BABY BEETS

Cut tops from 1 bunch small tender beets, remove root ends, wash. Place whole beets on heavy duty foil with 2 tablespoons water, sprinkling of salt. Seal foil into a tight package, place in 350°F oven. Bake 1¼ hours. Open, remove skins, add butter or margarine, and seasonings.

BUTTERED SLICED BEETS

Peel 1 bunch tender young beets; slice thinly and place in center of square of heavy duty foil. Add 2 tablespoons butter or marga-rine, 2 tablespoons lemon juice, 1 teaspoon sugar, salt and pepper. Bring foil up over beets; seal to make tight package. Bake in 350°F oven 1 hour.

GREEN BEANS WITH MUSHROOMS AND ONIONS

(4 servings)

1 pound green beans	*2 tablespoons butter or*
1 small onion, diced	*margarine*
¼ pound mushrooms,	*2 tablespoons water*
sliced	*Salt and pepper*

Snip beans diagonally into small, easily cooked pieces. Place in center of square of heavy duty foil and add all other ingredients. Bring foil up over vegetables, seal to make tight package. Bake in 350°F oven 40 minutes.

CARROTS IN FOIL

Scrape one bunch carrots and leave whole, or slice or cut in julienne strips. For 4 medium-size carrots, add 3 tablespoons water, 2 tablespoons butter, a generous sprinkling of salt and pepper. Seal in a tight package of heavy duty foil and place in a 350°F oven. Bake whole medium-size carrots 1½ hours, sliced or julienne carrots 1 hour.

POTATOES CHANTILLY *(4 servings)*

4 medium-size potatoes
½ cup heavy cream
3 tablespoons butter or margarine
¾ teaspoon salt
Generous grinding of pepper

2 tablespoons chopped parsley
½ cup grated sharp cheese

Peel and cut potatoes into thin strips as for French fries. Place in center of large piece of heavy duty foil. Pour the cream over, dot with the butter and sprinkle with seasonings, parsley and cheese. Bring foil up over potatoes; seal edges to make tight package. Place on cookie sheet and bake in 400°F oven for 40 minutes. Place package in a basket and serve right in Reynolds Wrap. Potatoes will be deliciously soft, the cream and cheese practically absorbed.

WAIT-A-WHILE POTATOES

Foil-bake potatoes. Cut lengthwise in 2 pieces, allowing ⅔ for the lower half. Scoop out centers and whip to feathery lightness with hot milk, butter, and seasonings. Add any of the following: finely cut ham cubes, cooked diced sausage, crisp bacon bits, small cubes of cheese. Heap the filling nicely in the larger potato-skin shell, discarding the smaller one. Sprinkle with paprika and melted butter. Wrap these stuffed potatoes in foil. Refrigerate for 1 or 2 days, or freeze. When ready to serve, place chilled potatoes in 400°F oven and heat 35 minutes. Turn back foil 5 minutes before done to brown lightly. If frozen, heat 10 minutes longer.

SWEET POTATO PUFFS

Cut 6 foil-baked sweet potatoes in two as above. Scoop out centers and mash. Add ¼ cup molasses, 2 tablespoons butter, a little nutmeg and salt, ½ cup milk, and 1 unbeaten egg. Whip up light and fill potato shells with mixture. Dot with butter. Flute foil to form attractive holders. Bake in 400°F oven until lightly browned. These Puffs may be frozen and baked just before serving.

SAVORY BROILED TOMATOES

Cut tomatoes in half and arrange in foil pan. Brush cut surfaces with melted butter or margarine and sprinkle with salt, pepper, a little garlic salt, and herbs if desired. Broil until beginning to soften and brown. Sprinkle with crumbs and cheese, or spread with equal parts of dairy sour cream and mayonnaise mixed with just a hint of curry powder. Continue to broil until lightly browned.

OVEN-ROASTED CORN ON THE COB

Husk corn, remove silk, and place each ear on square of heavy duty foil. Brush with melted butter or margarine; season with salt and pepper. Sprinkle with herbs or brush with barbecue sauce for extra flavor. Bring foil up over corn and seal lengthwise edges with double fold. Twist or crimp ends to secure. Bake in a 400°F oven 35 minutes. Delicious—no flavor wasted!

EGGPLANT PARMIGIANA   *(6 to 8 servings)*

6 or 8 small eggplants,   *1 small clove garlic,*
about 4 inches long   *crushed*
½ cup olive oil   *Salt and pepper*
3 8-ounce cans tomato   *1 cup grated Parmesan*
sauce   *cheese*
1 small onion, grated

Cut the eggplants in half lengthwise. Heat the olive oil in a skillet and sauté the eggplant halves lightly until just beginning to soften. Arrange layer in a foil-lined casserole, top with half the tomato sauce, sprinkle with half the seasonings and half the cheese. Repeat eggplant layer, topping with remaining sauce, seasonings and cheese. Bake in 350°F oven 25 minutes, or until the eggplants are tender.

99

Green Stuff

Green Stuff

New salad ideas, better ways with the old ones—
to eat with a meal or as the main course

Care of salad greens: If they are to be stored for a week or longer—
or if you are in a hurry—simply remove tough, outside leaves, rinse
with water and store in vegetable crisper. Bulky items should be
wrapped in foil and stored on refrigerator shelf.

When time permits, thoroughly prepare greens for salad . . .
enough to last for a few days. For a fine, tossed green salad, use only
the tenderest, center parts of two or three different greens. The
outer leaves may be cooked with spinach or turnip greens to add
extra flavor to those vegetables.

Rinse greens in several waters, then drain. Use a sharp knife to
cut the greens into pieces the right size for popping into the mouth
without further cutting. Place a linen napkin, dish towel or cheesecloth on a large square of foil. Place the greens on this and seal the
foil to form a tight package. Shake the package gently to remove
remaining drops of water. Store on refrigerator shelf, being sure
to chill for at least an hour—preferably longer—before using. The
cloth absorbs excess moisture and the foil keeps the greens ready
for use for several days.

Salad know-how: Everyone should know how to make a good green
salad. This is the simplest go-with-everything salad and also the
most sophisticated.

The famous old Ritz Carlton Hotel in New York, now torn down,
but fondly remembered for wonderful food, always served the most
delicious, delicately tender and subtly dressed green salad, of only
one or two different types of salad greens—usually Boston lettuce
and the tender heart of chicory—very cold and crisp, tossed with a
lightly garlic-perfumed oil-and-vinegar dressing.

Markets today offer a wonderful variety of greens and vegetables
to choose from in making salads. You can keep them ready for instant tossing into a salad with the help of Reynolds Wrap.

In color picture: Green Salad

PERFECT GREEN SALAD

Choose two or more varieties of fresh young greens. Here are the ones you will find most frequently in food markets:

Boston lettuce, sometimes called "butter" lettuce. This is a loose head of very tender, easily separated leaves. It has delicate flavor.

Iceberg lettuce, also called Simpson lettuce. This is most commonly available, is very tight and compact. It is very crisp and bland.

Bibb lettuce or limestone lettuce. This is a small head of loose, richly green lettuce with very tender, delicately flavored leaves. It is becoming quite generally available in metropolitan areas and is considered a gourmet green. Foil-wrap separately in crisper.

Belgian endive is the lovely, long, pale yellow tissue-paper wrapped bud packed in boxes. It is another gourmet green with a delicate, nut-like, slightly bitter flavor.

Chicory is the loose, large head of twisted, curly, slim green leaves. It should have a pale yellow center with lots of tiny, tender little leaves. It has a refreshing bitter flavor.

Escarole is the large, loose head of broad, long green leaves with a pale yellow center. Center leaves are tender, almost sweet and nutlike in flavor and are excellent in tossed salads. Outer leaves should be shredded.

Romaine is the large, long, almost celery-shaped head of rather coarse, pale green leaves. It has a pleasantly bitter flavor and the center leaves are very good in salads.

Watercress is easy to recognize by its rich, dark small green leaves. Sold tied together in bunches, it has a peppery taste. Be sure leaves are green and that the bunches are not broken or damaged. Handle gently when washing it, wrap separately in foil and refrigerate. Use within two to three days.

There are many other greens sold seasonally in markets. Tender leaves of young dandelions, spinach, field salad—all can be used. Using unusual salad greens marks you as an imaginative cook.

Making the salad: Choose a salad bowl that will fit in the refrigerator for chilling. The dressing may be made right in the bowl. If made in the bowl, place greens over dressing, cover with foil and refrigerate. Just before serving, toss lightly.

When making a very large amount of salad, it is better to refrigerate the greens alone in the salad bowl; make the dressing separately in a small dish or bowl. Cover it with foil, then pour over the greens and toss just at the moment of serving.

The dressing: French dressing made with oil and vinegar only, is nicest on a green salad. Use a variety of greens with hearty main courses, add additional ingredients when meal is light.

FRENCH DRESSING   *(6 servings)*

> 1 small clove garlic   6 tablespoons olive oil or
> 1 teaspoon salt   salad oil
> Generous grinding of
>   pepper
> 2 tablespoons wine,
>   malt, tarragon or
>   herb-flavored vinegar

Peel the garlic, then cut in snips with a sharp knife. Place garlic and salt in bowl and crush with back of a tablespoon, or crush on a cutting board with the flat side of a knife; scrape up and put in bowl. Add the other ingredients, stirring with a fork to mix flavors.

Salad tips: If possible, don't make dressing more than an hour or two before salad is to be tossed. Garlic tastes best when freshly snipped or crushed. Have individual bowls or plates well chilled for serving the salad. Some people like to make quite a to-do over preparing and tossing salad right at the table for the family and guests to enjoy. Bring the bowl of greens covered with foil, a big pepper grinder, oil, vinegar and other seasonings—all on a tray—to the table. Make the dressing in a small bowl at the table, pour it over the greens and toss with flourish. It tastes even better when you see it made!

To add to green salad:

Crumbled Roquefort cheese.

Fresh tomatoes—put in peeled, seeded, diced tomatoes on the last toss, or whole, small cherry tomatoes. (Use wedges or slices as garnish, but don't toss with greens, as this makes salad watery.)

Avocado, peeled and sliced—add at the last toss or use as garnish.

Artichoke bottoms, canned, drained. Add at last toss.

Thinly sliced radishes, cucumber, green pepper, carrot, onions.

Herbs, packaged dried or fresh. Herb blends for salads are sold in food markets. Dried herbs should be allowed to stand in dressing for an hour to give out their flavor. One teaspoon will flavor salad for 6. Fresh herbs—tarragon, dill, chives, fennel and basil —are particularly good. Snip them, using 2 teaspoons of combined herbs in salad for 6.

HEARTY CHEF'S SALAD   *(8 servings)*

2 quarts chilled greens in bite-size pieces

¾ cup of French dressing, well-seasoned with garlic and herbs

1½ cups of finely sliced Swiss or American cheese, ham, chicken or turkey and tongue, combined

This is a whole-meal salad and very delicious. Almost any combination of cheese and cold meats may be used, but they should be cut in very thin strips so they are not heavy. Chopped hard-cooked egg may also be added. Refrigerate all ingredients covered with foil, add dressing and toss just before serving.

POTATO SALAD   *(6 servings)*

1½ quarts sliced or diced cooked potatoes

½ cup or more French dressing

1 teaspoon grated onion
OR
2 tablespoons chopped chives or scallions

Salt and pepper to taste

1½ teaspoons chopped fresh herbs OR

1 teaspoon dried mixed salad herbs

Add, if you wish, one or more of these:

½ cup diced celery

2 to 3 hard-cooked eggs, diced

½ cup diced pimento

½ cup diced green pepper

½ cup mayonnaise

½ cup dairy sour cream

There are many ways to make potato salad. Choose good boiling potatoes that will not fall apart when cooked. New potatoes or California long whites are excellent. Cook in salted water until tender, cool slightly, then peel and dice or cut in ¼-inch slices. Place them in a bowl and, while still warm, pour the French dressing over. Toss lightly and, when dressing is absorbed, add onion or chives and herbs. If mayonnaise is not being used, add enough French dressing so that all potatoes are moistened with it. This may be served warm sprinkled with chopped parsley and is delicious with hot boiled ham, tongue, German sausages. For a creamy salad, add dressing, cool potatoes, then fold in mayonnaise—sour cream, too, if desired. If you want lots of color in the salad, fold in other ingredients listed. Cover with foil and refrigerate for an hour or longer to blend flavors, then serve on a bed of greens and garnish with cherry tomatoes.

MOLDED SALADS

The molded salad made with gelatin is excellent for party luncheons, buffets and any occasion when a colorful salad requiring no last-minute preparation is needed.

Foil can help with these salads. If they are to be molded in a ring or other shaped mold, use inch-wide strips of foil placed inside mold and extending above rim about three inches apart to aid in removing the salad. For individual molds, use a single half-inch strip of foil. Usually, it will not be necessary to dip the mold in hot water. Simply run the tip of the knife around top edges, then gently shake salad away from sides, letting a little air down between salad and mold on all sides. Tug on the foil to further loosen, then invert over greens and salad plate.

MOLDED SEAFOOD SALAD *(6 servings)*

1 envelope unflavored
  gelatin
¾ cup cold water
½ teaspoon salt
2 tablespoons lemon
  juice
¼ teaspoon Tabasco
¾ cup mayonnaise or
  salad dressing

1 cup finely diced celery
¼ cup finely diced
  green pepper
¼ cup chopped pimento
1 cup flaked or finely cut
  seafood (tuna, salmon,
  crabmeat, lobster or
  shrimp)

Sprinkle gelatin on cold water in saucepan to soften. Place over low heat, stirring constantly, until gelatin is dissolved. Remove from heat; stir in salt, lemon juice and Tabasco. Cool. Gradually stir into mayonnaise until blended. Mix in remaining ingredients. Turn into a 3-cup mold or 6 individual molds prepared as above. Cover with foil and chill until firm. Unmold on salad greens.
Another way: 1 cup of diced cooked chicken, turkey, or eggs (4 hard-cooked eggs) may be substituted for the seafood.

THOSE MARVELOUS CALIFORNIA SALADS

In California, salads are very often served as a first course. There, salads are hearty and topped with creamy rich salad dressing.

Make California-type salads an hour or two ahead, cover with Reynolds Wrap, chill. Top with dressing at the last minute.

CRAB LOUIS   *(4 servings)*

1 pound crabmeat
Salad greens
4 tomatoes
4 hard-cooked eggs
1 cup mayonnaise
¼ cup dairy sour cream
¼ cup chili sauce

¼ cup chopped green
   pepper
¼ cup chopped scallions
   OR mild onion
Salt and freshly ground
   pepper

Remove shell and membrane from crabmeat and arrange on lettuce or other salad greens. Cut tomatoes in wedges and eggs in quarters and arrange around crabmeat. Fold the mayonnaise, sour cream, chili sauce, green pepper and scallions together gently and add salt and pepper to taste. Spoon dressing over the salad.

Good to know: Alaskan King Crab is generally used for this salad.

It is the dressing that makes and gives its name to Green Goddess Salad. The dressing may be used on a salad made just of greens, tomato wedges and other flavorful vegetables, or it may be used on a chicken, or a shrimp or other seafood salad.

GREEN GODDESS DRESSING

1 small can anchovies,
   drained
1 small clove garlic
4 small scallions,
   chopped, OR
2 tablespoons chopped
   mild onion
2 tablespoons chopped
   parsley

1 tablespoon fresh OR
1 teaspoon dried
   tarragon
2 tablespoons tarragon
   vinegar
1½ cups mayonnaise
1 cup dairy sour cream

Place the first 6 ingredients in an electric blender and blend for one minute or until finely chopped. If you don't have a blender, mince these ingredients very fine, then combine with the vinegar. Fold the mayonnaise and sour cream together, then fold in the anchovy mixture. Cover with foil and refrigerate an hour or longer to blend flavors.

Meal-in-a-Dish Dining

Meal-in-a-Dish Dining

A simple trick—and in minutes you can serve delicious casserole meals that ought to take hours to prepare

Casseroles are the mainstay of party and buffet menus. They require no carving; guests can serve themselves and the food can usually be eaten with just a fork. Stored in the freezer, they are wonderful to have on hand for spur-of-the-moment entertaining and for emergencies when something delectable and hot is in order and there's no time to prepare it.

Reynolds Wrap has some very fine uses in casserole cookery. Here they are:

Line casseroles: Use Heavy Duty Reynolds Wrap. This prevents food from cooking on and forming a hard crust, difficult to clean off. Turn casserole upside down, mold foil on outside, turn, fit inside, pressing it to conform to shape of dish. Crimp edge around rim of dish to make attractive border.

Cover casseroles: Many beautiful casserole dishes are coverless. Foil forms a fine cover—it can be adjusted to just the right degree of tightness, and can be removed and put back with ease.

Make a casserole dish: When the right baking dish is lacking, line a 3-inch-deep roasting or other pan with heavy duty foil. Assemble ingredients in this and cover with foil. The cover may be crimped to the liner for an airtight seal. To serve, the pan may be put on a tray, surrounded with parsley, and the foil attractively crimped. This is great when very large amounts of food must be prepared for parties.

Freeze casseroles: Here is an excellent foil technique for freezing casseroles. Line the dish as above, fill with food, cook, cool, cover tightly with foil and freeze. When the food is firm, remove foil-enclosed frozen block of food. Make sure the foil is tightly sealed, label, and return to the freezer. The casserole dish goes back on the shelf ready for use. When time comes to serve the food, it will fit back into the original casserole for reheating.

In color picture: Creamy Rich Macaroni and Cheese

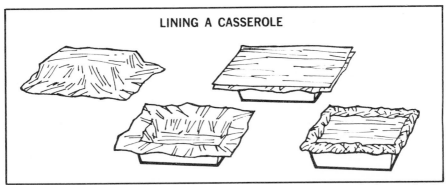

LINING A CASSEROLE

Freezing tips: When freezing casseroles, try to use dishes which are not too deep, because the frozen food, if very thick, takes longer to thaw. . . . Double the recipe of favorite casseroles. Serve one right away and freeze the other. . . . Use frozen casseroles within 3 months for best flavor.

Reheating frozen casseroles: Reheat from the frozen state, placing food back in the original casserole dish. Keep the food covered with foil so flavors will not escape. Preheat oven to 325°F. Allow 1½ hours for 2 quarts of a meat or poultry and vegetable with sauce.

FLEMISH BEER AND BEEF CASSEROLE
(14 to 16 servings)

1½ pounds onions,
   thinly sliced
2 cloves garlic, minced
¾ cup butter or oil
4 pounds round steak,
   cubed
½ cup flour
3 teaspoons salt
Generous grating of
   pepper

4 sprigs parsley
½ teaspoon nutmeg
½ teaspoon thyme
2 bay leaves
6 cups light beer
1½ tablespoons light
   brown sugar

In a large aluminum skillet, sauté the onions and garlic in 4 tablespoons of the butter or oil until golden. Trim fat from meat, dredge meat in the flour mixed with 2 teaspoons of the salt and pepper. Remove onions from pan and brown meat well, adding remaining butter or oil as needed. Line two 2-quart casseroles with heavy duty foil and place the meat in them. Spread the onions, garlic and parsley over meat and sprinkle with remaining herbs.

Pour off any fat remaining in skillet; add the beer and brown sugar. Heat, stirring in any brown residue. Add remaining 1 teaspoon salt, another sprinkling of pepper; pour over beef and vegetables. Cover and bake at 325°F about 2 hours, or until meat is tender. Remove from oven, remove bay leaf and parsley. Serve one casserole, cool and freeze the other.

Great go-withs: Serve boiled new potatoes and more beer.

CHICKEN DIVAN PARISIEN *(8 servings)*

2 3-pound broiler-fryers	4 peppercorns
OR	1 large bunch broccoli OR
1 6-pound roasting	2 pounds fresh asparagus
chicken	6 tablespoons butter
5 cups boiling water	6 tablespoons flour
1½ teaspoons salt	1 cup cream
1 small onion, cut in	½ cup grated Parmesan
quarters	cheese
1 stalk celery with leaves	Paprika
3 sprigs parsley	

Cook the chicken in the boiling water to which next 5 ingredients have been added. Remove it from the bones and cut in convenient serving pieces. Strain and remove fat from broth. Prepare the broccoli or asparagus very carefully so it will cook through evenly: cut off tough end of stems; remove skin from lower part of stems; slit up through thick broccoli stems for quick cooking. Cook in boiling salted water until barely tender. Drain; turn out on cheesecloth or towel to dry.

Line two 2-quart casseroles with heavy duty foil and arrange the broccoli or asparagus in them in rows so that it will be easy to serve later. Arrange the chicken on top. Cover and keep warm. Melt the butter in a large skillet; stir in the flour and cook 3 minutes without browning. Add 4 cups of hot broth, stirring constantly. Cook until smooth and thickened. Add the cream, additional seasonings to taste. Pour over the chicken. Sprinkle with the cheese and paprika. Bake one casserole at 375°F for 20 minutes or until the top is slightly browned, mixture bubbling. Cool and freeze second casserole.

For very special occasions: Use 4 whole chicken breasts instead of whole chickens. Simmer in canned or homemade chicken broth and seasonings. Continue recipe as above.

Turkey Divan: Slices of roast turkey may be substituted for chicken, using enough turkey to make 8 servings and arranging it evenly over the vegetable. Use turkey broth or canned or home-made chicken broth for sauce.

FABULOUS CHICKEN AND MUSHROOM CASSEROLE
(12 servings)

3 3-pound broiler-fryers, cut up
4 cups chicken broth
½ cup butter or margarine
18 very small white onions
2 small cloves garlic, finely minced
1 pound mushrooms, cut in quarters
6 tablespoons Minute Tapioca
1 teaspoon salt
Freshly ground pepper
Chopped parsley

Place chicken backs, wing tips and giblets in a kettle with 4 cups of chicken broth (or water and seasonings). Simmer for 40 minutes, adding a little water occasionally if necessary. This should give you about 4 cups of full-flavored chicken broth. Melt the butter in a skillet; quickly brown the remaining chicken. Arrange in two casseroles. In the same skillet, sauté the onions and garlic and place around chicken. Sauté the mushrooms about ⅓ at a time, adding more butter if needed, and arrange over the chicken. Pour off any fat remaining in skillet. Combine chicken broth, tapioca, salt and pepper in the skillet, cook, stirring constantly until thickened. Pour this over the chicken in the casseroles. Cover and bake at 325°F for 1 hour or until chicken is tender. Test with a fork. Serve one casserole topped with chopped parsley, cool and freeze the other.

CREAMY RICH MACARONI AND CHEESE   *(10 servings)*

1 8-ounce package elbow or shell macaroni
½ cup butter or margarine
2 tablespoons chopped onion
¼ pound fresh mushrooms, sliced
4 tablespoons flour
3 cups milk, heated
1 10-ounce package American cheese, grated
1 teaspoon salt
⅛ teaspoon each: paprika, pepper

Cook macaroni as package directs. Melt half the butter in a good-size aluminum skillet and sauté onions and mushrooms quickly. Lift out and reserve. Add remaining butter to skillet, melt, add flour, and stir and cook without browning for 3 minutes. Add hot milk, stir and cook until smooth and thickened. Add 2½ cups of the cheese and seasonings. Stir over low heat until thoroughly blended. Drain macaroni. Line two 1½-quart casseroles with heavy duty foil. Arrange layers of macaroni, onions, mushrooms and sauce in each. Repeat, topping final layer with the ½ cup cheese. Bake one casserole in a 400°F oven until lightly browned. Serve . Thoroughly cool the second and freeze.

Good to know: Leftover ham or tongue, cut into small cubes, is delicious in this casserole.

VEAL MARENGO   *(16 servings)*

4 pounds shoulder of veal	2 cups canned tomato sauce OR
3 tablespoons olive oil	4 medium tomatoes, peeled, seeded, chopped
1 clove garlic, minced	
1 pound sliced mushrooms	1 cup dry white wine
20 small white onions	2 cups fresh or canned chicken broth
4 tablespoons flour	
2½ teaspoons salt	Bouquet garni (celery, parsley, thyme, bay leaf)
½ teaspoon freshly ground black pepper	

Cut the veal in 1½-inch cubes. Heat the olive oil in a large skillet with the garlic. Brown veal, placing just enough in the skillet at one time to cover the bottom. Line two 2-quart casseroles with heavy duty foil. Place the veal in the casseroles, dividing it equally. Add a little additional oil to the skillet, if necessary; brown the mushrooms very quickly and lightly, and remove; then brown the onions. Arrange over meat. Stir the flour and seasonings into remaining oil in skillet. Add tomato sauce or tomatoes. Add wine and broth. Cook, stirring constantly, until thickened and smooth. Pour over veal mixture. Add to each casserole a herb bouquet (bouquet garni) of a 3-inch celery stalk with leaves, 2 sprigs parsley, a bay leaf, and a bit of fresh thyme. Tie together with stem of the parsley. Cover casseroles; bake at 325°F 1¼ hours. Remove herb bouquets. Serve one casserole; cool and freeze the second.

VEAL PARMIGIANA *(6 servings)*

1½ pounds veal cutlets
⅓ cup flour
1 teaspoon salt
Generous grating of
   pepper
½ cup butter, margarine
   OR olive oil
2 onions, minced
1 clove garlic, minced

1½ cups canned tomato
   sauce
½ teaspoon sugar
¼ teaspoon each:
   rosemary, thyme
¼ cup grated Parmesan
   cheese
½ pound Mozzarella
   cheese

Cut the veal cutlets in serving-size pieces; if they are not thin, pound them with the edge of a strong plate to ¼-inch thickness. Add a little salt and pepper to the flour and coat the cutlets, shaking off excess. Heat the butter or oil in a large skillet. Sauté the cutlets a few at a time, browning on both sides. Line a shallow casserole with heavy duty foil and place the cutlets in it. Add the onions and garlic to the skillet and sauté them until tender and light yellow. Add the tomato sauce, sugar, herbs and salt and pepper. Simmer a few minutes. Push the veal to one side of the casserole and pour about ⅔ cup of the tomato sauce into the bottom; arrange cutlets over it. Top with the Mozzarella slices and pour remaining sauce over. Sprinkle with the Parmesan. Bake at 350°F until the cheese is melted and the sauce bubbling. Double the recipe; bake in two casseroles—serve one, freeze the other.

Fresh From the Oven

Fresh From the Oven

*Make store-bought bread taste as if you'd baked it—
or start from scratch. This chapter makes either way easy*

There's bread to meet every taste in markets today—wonderful loaves delivered fresh daily. It's so good, it deserves special care after it reaches your kitchen. Store bread in a well-ventilated bread drawer or bread box. Don't crowd and don't crush. If it is to be kept for longer than 3 or 4 days, overwrap the bread in Reynolds Wrap and store in the freezer.

Contrary to what most people think, bread will not keep fresh for days on end in the refrigerator. But it will keep for 6 to 8 weeks in the freezer if given the extra protection of foil.

Be sure to keep frozen coffee cakes and other frozen breads in the freezer until needed, then thaw and warm. Use immediately or within 1 or 2 days. If bread products do become stale, it helps to wrap them in foil and heat in a 350°F oven for 15 to 20 minutes. Many types of bread, rolls and biscuits taste best if briefly heated. Wrap them loosely in Reynolds Wrap and heat in 350°F oven for 10 to 15 minutes.

THINGS TO DO WITH BREAD YOU BUY

Emergency Garlic Bread: Use a standard loaf of favorite white bread. Soften ¼ pound butter, add ½ teaspoon garlic salt, 2 tablespoons parsley flakes or chopped frozen chives. Blend thoroughly, then spread lightly on bread slices. As you spread, pile slices one on top of the other on large sheet of foil. When all bread is spread, turn so that slices are back in original loaf shape. Bring foil up around the bread, mitering corners to make a box-like container that holds bread loosely upright. Spread leftover seasoned butter lightly over top crust. Place the bread in 375°F oven and bake 20 minutes, or until bread looks crisp on top. To serve, place foil-boxed bread on tray or in bread basket.

In color picture: Supper-on-a-Slice

Parmesan Loaf: Add ½ cup grated Parmesan cheese to butter; prepare as above. Sprinkle top crust with a little paprika.

Hot Roll Fancies: Use clover leaf or fan-tan rolls (these separate into several little slices). Place rolls on foil and open them up. Spread with softened butter or margarine to which any one of the following has been added: poppy seeds, packaged mixed herbs blended for salads, crushed fresh garlic, Parmesan cheese.

Miniature Garlic Loaves: These are good for parties—also good if the family is small. Simply slice crusty French rolls in little ½-inch slices, or cut in half, first lengthwise, then across. Don't go completely through bottom crust. Spread with garlic butter or any flavor additions above.

Crusty loaves of French or Italian bread are delicious fresh from the bakery. Usually sold without wrapping, they should be foil-wrapped if kept for a second day. Heat these crusty loaves loosely wrapped in foil in 350°F oven about 10 minutes to fully develop flavor. Serve right in foil, in a long bread basket. Close foil up around bread after first serving to keep it warm.

HERBED ITALIAN BREAD

1 loaf Italian bread
(12 to 14 inches long)
¼ pound soft butter or
margarine
¼ teaspoon oregano

1 clove garlic, crushed
1 teaspoon parsley flakes
4 tablespoons grated
Parmesan cheese

Cut bread diagonally in ¾-inch slices, almost but not quite through the bottom crust. Combine butter or margarine with oregano, garlic, parsley flakes and spread on both sides of each bread slice. Place bread on long piece of foil, shaping the foil around sides. Combine any remaining butter mixture with Parmesan cheese and spread on top of loaf. Heat in 400° oven or on outdoor grill 15 minutes.

JIM'S FAVORITE GARLIC BREAD

Prepare French or Italian bread as for Herbed Italian Bread. Spread with ¼ pound softened butter or margarine blended with 1 crushed clove garlic and ¼ cup chopped fresh parsley. Heat in 400°F oven or on outdoor grill 15 minutes.

To Freeze Prepared Garlic Bread and Other Flavored Loaves: Wrap and seal in heavy duty foil. To serve, place direct from freezer in 375° oven or on outdoor grill and heat 30 minutes. Open foil at top of loaf during last 10 minutes to crisp crust.

SUPPER-ON-A-SLICE   *(6 servings)*

1½ pounds ground beef
1 small can undiluted evaporated milk
½ cup soft stale bread crumbs
1 egg
½ cup finely chopped onion
1 teaspoon prepared mustard

1½ teaspoons salt
⅛ teaspoon pepper
1 cup grated American cheese
1 loaf Italian or French bread
4 slices natural or process American cheese, cut into strips

Combine all ingredients except the bread loaf and sliced cheese. Cut the bread in half lengthwise. Place each half, crust side down, on foil sheet 1½ inches larger all around than bread. Spread meat mixture evenly over bread. Bring foil up around each bread half, crimping together at ends to form boat-shaped holders. Bake in 350°F oven 25 minutes; arrange strips of cheese over tops and bake 5 minutes longer. To serve, cut bread across diagonally and accompany with catsup specially flavored for steak.

Stuffed buns are great for club luncheons, picnics and late suppers. Wrap in foil and store in refrigerator until needed. Or freeze them—they'll keep for 6 weeks sealed in foil, and can be heated without defrosting.

TUNA TEMPTIES   *(4 servings)*

¼ pound American cheese, cubed
1 7-ounce can tuna, flaked
2 tablespoons chopped green pepper
2 tablespoons minced onion

2 tablespoons chopped sweet pickle
¼ cup salad dressing
Salt and pepper
4 hamburger or frankfurter buns
Butter or margarine

Combine first 6 ingredients; season. Split buns, scoop out and discard the soft centers; spread with softened butter or margarine, and fill. Wrap buns in foil. Place on shallow pan and bake in 350°F oven for 15 minutes, until filling is heated and cheese melts. If frozen, allow 15 additional minutes of heating time. To heat on outdoor grill: place packages on grill over low fire and heat 30 minutes, turning once or twice. Serve hot.

Chicken or Turkey Buns: Substitute 1 cup diced cooked chicken or turkey for the tuna. Omit cheese.

Ham and Cheese Buns: Substitute ¾ cup diced cooked ham.

Puffy little refrigerated biscuits are one of the great blessings for families who like hot breads. You'll find it easy to flip them out onto a square of heavy duty foil for panless baking. You can dress them up, too, with a few extra ingredients for occasions when you want to make them special.

CHEESE-TOPPED BISCUITS *(8 to 10 servings)*

2 packages refrigerated biscuits

1 4-ounce package shredded sharp cheese

2 tablespoons light cream

½ teaspoon poppy seeds

⅛ teaspoon dry mustard

Arrange 15 biscuits, overlapping around outside edge of a foil-lined 9-inch round layer cake pan. Use remaining 5 biscuits to make inner circle of overlapping biscuits. Combine cheese, cream, poppy seeds and mustard; crumble evenly over top of biscuits. Bake at 425°F about 15 minutes. Remove from pan immediately.

DO-AHEAD POPOVERS *(8 popovers)*

2 eggs

1 cup milk

1 tablespoon melted butter or margarine

1 cup sifted flour

½ teaspoon salt

Press a 9-inch square of heavy duty foil into each of eight 5-ounce custard cups. Do not trim off excess foil. Grease foil cups. Beat eggs lightly with rotary beater or electric mixer. Beat in the milk and melted shortening, then gradually beat in flour and salt, beating until smooth. Divide batter among prepared cups and pull corners of foil together, crimping to seal. Store in freezer. When ready to bake, remove the desired number of packages from freezer, open, and shape foil to make straight high sides. Do not defrost. Place on shallow pan or cookie sheet. Bake in 425°F oven 20 minutes. Reduce heat to 325°F. Continue baking 35 to 40 minutes or until popovers are crisp and brown.

HOMEMADE BREAD—AN EASY WAY

Making bread is wonderful fun, and the kneading is excellent exercise for hands and arms—but it does take time. A streamlined method has been worked out by home economists with one of the large flour companies. Instant blending flour can be used, thus eliminating sifting, and the dough is mixed and formed into loaves or rolls right at the start. Instead of rising twice in a warm place, the shaped loaves are put in the refrigerator to rise slowly. They may be baked any time after 2 hours and up to 24 hours. This method produces excellent bread without the bother of handling the dough twice, and the bread may be baked when convenient.

It is important to use a high gluten flour for all yeast-raised breads to supply elasticity for rising. Generally, all flour sold in 10-pound bags has high gluten content. Five-pound bags frequently have lower gluten content. They are most often purchased for cake making and other uses requiring smaller amounts of flour.

COOL-RISE BREAD *(2 loaves)*

5½ to 6½ cups all-purpose or instant blending flour
½ cup warm water (105 to 115°F)
2 packages or cakes yeast, active dry or compressed

1¾ cups warm milk (105 to 115°F)
2 tablespoons sugar
1 tablespoon salt
3 tablespoons butter or margarine
Cooking oil

Spoon or pour flour into dry measuring cup. Level off and pour measured flour onto dry foil.

Measure warm water into large warm bowl. Sprinkle or crumble in yeast; stir until dissolved. Add warm milk, sugar, salt and butter. Stir in 2 cups flour. Beat with electric mixer until smooth (about 1 minute). Add 1 cup flour and continue beating 5 minutes. Remove beaters and add enough additional flour by hand to make a soft dough. Turn out onto a lightly floured board and knead until smooth and elastic, 5 to 10 minutes. Cover with foil. Let rest on board 20 minutes.

Punch down; divide dough in half. With rolling pin, roll each portion into an 8 x 12 inch rectangle. Beginning with upper 8-inch edge, roll dough toward you. Seal with thumbs or heel of hand after each complete turn. Seal final seam and edges well. Place in 2 greased loaf pans (8½ x 4½ x 2½ inch size). Brush with oil. Cover pans loosely with foil. Refrigerate 2 to 24 hours.

When ready to bake, remove loaves from refrigerator. Carefully uncover the dough; let stand for 10 minutes at room temperature. Using a greased toothpick or metal skewer, puncture any surface bubbles that may have formed on the dough.

Bake in 400°F oven 30 to 40 minutes, or until done. Brush tops with melted butter or margarine.

Raisin bread: Add 2 cups raisins by hand at end of electric mixer beating period.

OLD FASHIONED REFRIGERATOR ROLLS   *(4 dozen)*

¾ cup hot water
½ cup sugar
1 tablespoon salt
3 tablespoons butter or
  margarine
1 cup warm water

2 packages or cakes
  yeast, active dry or
  compressed
1 egg, beaten
5¼ cups unsifted
  all-purpose flour

Mix together hot water, sugar, salt and shortening in a small bowl. Cool to lukewarm. Measure warm water into large warm bowl. Sprinkle or crumble in the yeast; stir until dissolved. Stir in lukewarm water mixture, egg, and half the flour; beat until smooth. Stir in enough remaining flour to make a soft dough. Turn out onto lightly floured board and knead until smooth and elastic—about 10 minutes. Place dough in a greased bowl, turning so top is greased, and cover tightly with foil. Store in refrigerator until doubled in bulk; if not used at once, it will keep 3 to 4 days in refrigerator at 40°. To use, punch down and cut off amount of dough needed. This dough may be used to form pan rolls or any type desired.

PARKERHOUSE ROLLS: Roll out dough ½ inch thick. Cut with 2-inch cookie cutter into rounds. Dough left over may be kneaded and rolled again until it is all used. Brush each round with melted butter. With the dull side of a knife, make a deep indentation across the center of each round and fold in half. Place in foil-lined pan ¼ inch apart. Brush tops with a little melted butter. Cover with foil and let rise until doubled in bulk. Bake in 400°F oven 15 minutes or until golden brown. If rolls open up, just push two halves together again.

Banquets in Bundles

Banquets in Bundles

A brand-new idea, a little planning, one quick twist of the foil—and you're ready for any occasion

Most of us enjoy cooking—but oh, the cleaning up afterwards! How many times have we wished for a method of cooking that would eliminate the need for washing up after a delicious dinner!

Well, here it is—the secret lies in lining all pans with foil. This is not tedious, painstaking lining, but just a quick fitting of heavy duty foil inside a broiler pan, a large shallow casserole, cake or any pan that will hold the food. Use foil as a cover.

You may worry that this is expensive, but it is not. The cost of hot water, detergents, and scouring aids about equals the cost of a piece of foil—to say nothing of saving time and wear and tear.

Here are recipes and suggestions for easy meals—things that quite literally can be put into the oven and forgotten until they are cooked, then served right from the foil. Others require a little more attention, but all need the use of few utensils other than Heavy Duty Reynolds Wrap.

If there are leftovers, place them right in the original foil in the refrigerator. To serve a second time, the package goes into the oven as is—again, no pan!

OVEN BEEF STEW *(6 servings)*

2 pounds tender beef, cut in 1½-inch cubes
2 tablespoons bottled steak sauce
1 10-ounce package frozen mixed vegetables, partially thawed
1 1-pound can tomatoes, drained
4 tablespoons instant blending flour
1 onion, finely chopped
2 teaspoons salt
Generous grating of pepper
½ teaspoon mixed herbs
1 package refrigerated biscuits

In color picture: Lamb Bundles

Line a large casserole or pan with heavy duty foil. Trim fat from meat; place meat in casserole. Brush with steak sauce. Add vegetables and tomatoes and sprinkle with the flour. Sprinkle with onion, salt, pepper, herbs. Use a second piece of foil to cover the food, sealing the foil to the liner by double-folding edges together. Bake in a 325°F oven 1½ hours. Remove cover, stir mixture lightly, then arrange refrigerated biscuits on top. Increase heat to 400°F and return casserole to the oven. Bake 15 minutes longer or until biscuits are brown.

Good to know: For still faster preparation, sprinkle the meat and vegetables with a 1¾-ounce envelope of beef or brown gravy mix. Omit the flour, salt, pepper, and herbs. If beef is not a tender cut, bake at 300°F for 2 hours before arranging biscuits.

EASY BLANQUETTE DE VEAU   (6 servings)

2 pounds veal cutlet or shoulder, cut in 1-inch pieces
½ pound fresh mushrooms OR
1 6-ounce can mushrooms, drained
3 medium carrots, cut in 1-inch lengths
6 small white onions

2 teaspoons salt
Generous grating of pepper
½ teaspoon mixed herbs
1 10¾-ounce can chicken gravy
3 tablespoons instant blending flour
½ pint dairy sour cream

Line a casserole or pan with heavy duty foil and arrange meat in it. Add mushrooms—whole if small, cut in quarters if large. Add carrots and onions. Sprinkle with the seasonings and pour the gravy over. Cover the food with a second piece of foil, sealing it to the liner. Bake in a 325°F oven for 1 hour. Remove from oven and turn back foil. Stir flour into sour cream and add to gravy, stirring just enough to blend. Cover and return to the oven for 15 minutes. Serve sprinkled with chopped parsley.

FAMILY STEAK   (6 servings)

2 pounds chuck or round steak, 1 inch thick
1 10½-ounce can mushroom gravy

1 can or envelope onion soup mix

Trim excess fat from meat. Place sheet of heavy duty foil on shallow pan and arrange meat in the center. Pour the mushroom gravy over and sprinkle with the onion soup mix. Bring edges of foil together; seal with double fold to make tight package. Bake in 325°F oven 2 hours.

Great go-withs: Cold seafood cocktail, foil-baked sweet potatoes, frozen vegetable baked in foil, Blueberry Pizza.

BLUEBERRY PIZZA

1 11-inch pie crust circle
1 package frozen
    blueberries
½ cup sugar
4 tablespoons
    instant blending flour

TOPPING:
½ cup sugar
½ teaspoon each:
    nutmeg, cinnamon
¾ cup flour
¼ cup butter or
    margarine

Use a frozen pastry circle from the freezer (page 151) or make up pastry from a mix. Place a circle of foil, a little larger all around than the pastry, on a cookie sheet. Place pastry on foil; turn up together all around edge to make a 1-inch-high rim. Pinch foil and pastry to make firm. Shake blueberries into the crust. Combine ½ cup sugar and instant blending flour. Sprinkle this over the berries, stirring so they are coated. Combine second ½ cup sugar, flour, spices and butter in a bowl, using the fingers to make a crumbly mixture. Sprinkle over berries. Bake in 425°F oven 25 minutes.

Good to know: Bake this "pizza" while the first course is being eaten; serve hot from the oven with whipped cream.

SWISS BLISS   (4 to 6 servings)

½ tablespoon butter or
    margarine
2 pounds chuck steak,
    cut 1-inch thick
1 envelope onion soup
    mix
½ pound mushrooms,
    sliced
½ green pepper, sliced
1 1-pound can tomatoes,
    drained and chopped

¼ teaspoon salt
Generous grating of
    pepper
½ cup juice from
    canned tomatoes
1 tablespoon bottled
    steak sauce
1 tablespoon cornstarch
2 tablespoons parsley

Place 20-inch sheet of heavy duty foil on a shallow pan. Spread center with butter or margarine. Cut steak into serving portions.

Arrange on foil, slightly overlapping portions. Sprinkle with onion soup mix, mushrooms, green pepper, tomatoes. Season. Mix juice, steak sauce and cornstarch. Pour over meat and vegetables. Bring foil up, seal tightly. Bake 2 hours at 350°F. Top with parsley.

LAMB BUNDLES (4 servings)

4 lamb shanks
4 tablespoons bottled
* steak sauce*
4 medium-size onions

4 tender carrots
Salt
Freshly ground pepper
Minced garlic (optional)

Purchase meaty lamb shanks, each sufficient for 1 serving. Trim off excess fat. Place each on large square of heavy duty foil. Brush with steak sauce. Add the vegetables—whole if they are small, cut in halves or quarters if larger. Divide them among the packages and sprinkle each serving with seasonings. Seal foil to make tight packages and place on shallow pan. Bake in 325°F oven 1½ hours. Serve packages on plates, letting each person open his own. Vegetables may be varied to suit family tastes.
Great go-withs: Partially thawed frozen fruit cocktail, cole slaw, Double Fudge Cake.

DOUBLE FUDGE CAKE (12 servings)

1 package devil's food
* cake mix*
1 cup chocolate
* mix*

1 cup heavy cream

Line a 13 x 9 inch pan with heavy duty foil. Prepare cake mix according to package directions. Pour into foil-lined pan. Bake in 325°F oven 35 minutes. Serve warm or cold topped with whipped cream flavored with chocolate drink mix.

BROILED DINNERS

Broil your dinner for really fast, fast preparation. Line the bottom pan of the broiler with heavy duty foil (page 32); arrange meat, poultry, or fish on the rack of the pan. Broil until nearly done, then arrange quick-cooking vegetables and fruits around the meat to brown and heat through. Even the rack of the broiler may be lined with foil, or it may be plunked into the dishwasher along with the dishes. Here are two quick broiler meals you'll enjoy!

BROILED HAM DINNER   (4 servings)

1 center ham slice,
  1 inch thick
2 tablespoons honey
4 tomatoes, cut in half
4 tablespoons melted
  butter or margarine
Salt and freshly ground
  pepper

1 8-ounce package
  frozen green beans in
  sauce
2 large bananas, cut in
  half
¼ cup Parmesan
  cheese, grated

Line broiler pan with heavy duty foil; preheat. Slash the ham fat at 1-inch intervals so that it won't curl; place ham on rack. Broil until lightly browned. Turn and brush with honey. Place tomatoes at one end of slice, brush with melted butter, sprinkle with seasonings. Return pan to heat and broil for 5 minutes longer. Meanwhile, cook green beans according to package directions. Turn into small pan formed from foil. Remove broiler pan; place beans at other end of ham slice, bananas around sides. Brush bananas with honey and butter; season tomatoes and beans, sprinkle with Parmesan, continue broiling 5 to 7 minutes, or until food is lightly browned. If desired, frozen potato puffs may be arranged around outer edge of broiler pan during the last part of broiling. Garnish with parsley.

When leg of lamb is a special at the market, have it cut in half and have 2 or more ¾-inch slices cut from the center. Use the shank end for braising or stew, the large end for roasting, and the center slices for broiling. A steak from a large lamb leg will serve 2 people.

BROILED LAMB STEAK DINNER   (4 servings)

2 center slices cut from
  leg of lamb
2½ cups diced cooked
  potatoes
2 tablespoons grated
  onion
Salt and pepper
4 small zucchini, cut in
  half lengthwise

4 tablespoons melted
  butter or margarine
4 tablespoons lemon juice
½ teaspoon thyme
½ teaspoon rosemary
4 halves canned cling
  peaches
4 tablespoons currant
  jelly

Trim most of fat from lamb and arrange slices on broiler pan rack. Line the bottom of the pan with heavy duty foil and put in the potatoes and onion. Season with salt and pepper. Place the broiler rack over the vegetables. Arrange the zucchini slices beside the lamb. Combine the melted butter with the lemon juice and herbs, brush on the lamb and zucchini and sprinkle both with salt and pepper. Broil until nicely brown on first side; turn and again brush with the lemon glaze and season. Fill peach halves with currant jelly and slide onto the broiler pan to brown when lamb is almost done.

Good to know: The lamb should be nicely brown on the outside, pink in the center. It should not take more than 10 or 12 minutes in all. Meat, vegetables, and fruit juices add extra flavor to the potatoes. If desired, as soon as the food is removed from the rack, place bottom pan with potatoes under broiler 2 to 3 minutes to brown lightly.

SIZZLING PLATTER DINNERS

Heatproof platters of aluminum, glass or ceramic materials provide another easy way of getting dinner on the table in a hurry—they go directly from broiler or oven to the table. Line them with foil—they will never need scrubbing.

FLAMBÉED CHICKEN BREAST DINNER   *(4 servings)*

*2 chicken breasts, split
   in half
4 tablespoons butter or
   margarine, melted
Salt and freshly ground
   pepper
1 15-ounce can
   artichoke hearts,
   drained*

*2 cups canned or
   cooked baby carrots,
   drained
1 package instant
   potatoes
4 tablespoons brandy*

Arrange chicken breasts cut side up on large heatproof platter lined with heavy duty foil. Brush with melted butter, sprinkle with the seasonings. Place under broiler heat and broil slowly about 15 minutes, or until nicely browned. Turn, brush second side with melted butter, sprinkle with seasonings, broil 10 minutes longer. Remove from heat, arrange artichoke hearts and carrots around chicken. Brush with melted butter and season. Return to broiler for 10 minutes. Prepare potatoes according to package directions; place spoonfuls around outer edge of platter. Again place under broiler—6 or more inches from the heat—and broil for 3 minutes longer, or until potatoes are lightly tinged with brown and chicken is golden. Warm the brandy and pour it over the chicken. Light it with a match and spoon brandy and pan juices over the chicken.

SIZZLING FISH DINNER   *(4 servings)*

4 thick fish fillets or steaks, fresh or frozen
4 tablespoons butter or margarine, melted
4 large mushrooms, stems removed
2 large tomatoes, cut in half
Salt, freshly ground pepper and paprika
2 tablespoons lemon juice
1 package frozen peas in cream sauce
2 cans shoe string potatoes
Parsley sprigs

Partially thaw frozen fish. Place a large piece of heavy duty foil on the rack of the broiler pan or in a shallow pan. Rub with a few drops of butter or margarine where fish will rest and place fish, mushroom caps and tomatoes on the foil. Brush with 2 tablespoons of the butter; sprinkle with all the seasonings and the lemon juice. Place under the broiler, broil 8 to 10 minutes or until about two-thirds done. Meanwhile, warm a heatproof platter and prepare peas according to package directions. Slide the foil with fish and vegetables onto platter. Turn fish. Turn up foil on all sides, crimping to make a pretty border. Fill the mushroom caps with creamed peas. Brush remaining butter, a little salt and pepper on the fish ; sprinkle on peas and tomatoes. Arrange shoe string potatoes around outer edge to make a border. Return platter to the broiler and continue broiling 4 to 5 minutes, or until fish begins to flake when tested with a fork and vegetables and potatoes are lightly browned. Decorate with parsley, bring proudly to the table.

DELECTABLE FOIL-BUNDLE DINNERS
FOR ONE OR TWO

When the family is small, it's easy to fix delicious individual dinners. Tear off rectangles of Heavy Duty Reynolds Wrap, about 12 x 18 inches. Arrange the food in the center, then seal the foil to make a tight package. Place packages on a cookie sheet or shallow pan and bake.

Fix these dinners ahead for Dad or other members of the family who must "get their own dinner" when you are out with the girls. Leave them in the refrigerator with a note attached giving cooking directions. Allow 10 minutes extra baking time if they are chilled.

Wonderful, tender, and savory, when cooked they are ready to eat—right out of the foil "bundle"!

LAMB CHOP OR PORK CHOP INDIVIDUAL DINNER: Slice a potato into the center of a square of heavy duty foil. Add several slices of onion and 2 tablespoons milk. Rub a shoulder lamb chop or pork chop with bottled meat sauce; arrange on potato. Sprinkle with salt and pepper. Top with 2 tablespoons condensed cream of mushroom soup; arrange a serving of frozen peas or other vegetables around sides. Bring foil up over food and seal to make a tight package. Place on shallow pan; bake in 325°F oven 1½ hours.

INDIVIDUAL BURGER DINNER: Prepare your favorite meat loaf recipe, allowing ⅓ pound meat per person. Shape each serving into a flat patty. Place on square of heavy duty foil. Cover with ½ cup canned kidney beans, drained. Spoon on 2 tablespoons bottled barbecue sauce and top with 2 slices fresh tomato. Bring foil up over food to make tight package, place on shallow pan and bake in 350°F oven 40 minutes.

CHICKEN-IN-FOIL DINNER: Use half or quarter or just a breast of a broiler-fryer, depending on the size of the bird. Place in the center of a square of heavy duty foil, skin side down. Brush with bottled steak sauce. Pour over chicken ½ can of condensed cream of mushroom, chicken, or celery soup. Add a serving of any canned or frozen vegetable. Bring foil up over food and seal to make a tight package. Place on shallow pan and bake in 350°F oven 50 to 60 minutes.

SHRIMP CELESTIAL: Arrange 8 medium shrimp, cleaned and deveined, in the center of 12-inch square of heavy duty foil. Top with 1 tablespoon chopped scallions, 8 to 10 thin slices each of canned water chestnuts and carrot. Sprinkle with ⅓ teaspoon salt, ¼ teaspoon minced garlic, and dot with 1 teaspoon butter or margarine. Bring foil up and pinch top to make a tight bag. Place in a saucepan containing 1 inch of boiling water; cover tightly and cook 15 minutes. Or place on a shallow pan and bake 15 to 20 minutes in a 400°F oven.

BAKED PORK CHOPS, APPLES AND SWEET POTATOES (6 servings)

6 pork chops, 1 inch
thick
Salt and pepper
Onion salt or flakes
6 apple rings, ½ inch
thick

6 medium sweet
potatoes, cooked and
sliced
¼ cup brown sugar
Sprinkling of nutmeg

Line a shallow casserole or pan with heavy duty foil. Trim excess fat from chops and arrange in the pan. Season well with salt and pepper and a little onion salt or flakes. Place in a 350°F oven and bake for 35 minutes or until lightly browned. Remove from oven, arrange an apple ring on each chop and the sweet potatoes around the chops. Sprinkle sweet potatoes and apple rings with brown sugar and nutmeg. Cover loosely and return to oven. Cook 20 minutes longer or until chops are almost tender. Remove foil and spoon drippings over food; bake 5 minutes longer.

CURRY-STUFFED PORK CHOP DINNER (4 servings)

4 double-thick pork
chops
Salt and freshly ground
pepper
1 cup packaged bread
stuffing mix
2 tablespoons melted
butter
2 tablespoons minced
onion

¼ cup finely diced
celery
¼ cup finely diced
apple
1 teaspoon curry
powder
Boiling water
4 small zucchini, sliced
Canned sweet potatoes
or yams

Trim excess fat from chops. Line a shallow baking dish or pan with heavy duty foil and place chops in center. Sprinkle well with salt and pepper; bake in 325°F oven for 30 minutes or until lightly browned and almost tender. While chops bake, combine the stuffing mix with butter, onion, celery, apple and curry powder, adding just enough boiling water to moisten. Cook zucchini until almost tender and drain. Drain sweet potatoes or yams. Remove chops from oven. Place spoonfuls of stuffing on each chop. Spoon out any fat in the pan, arrange the vegetables around the meat. Baste them with pan juices. Return to the oven and bake 15 to 20 minutes longer, or until chops are tender.

DELICIOUS LAMB CURRY   *(6 servings)*

2 pounds boneless lamb,
  cut in 1-inch cubes
3 small onions, sliced
1 cup chopped celery
2 tablespoons bottled
  steak sauce
1 tart apple, peeled and
  diced

1 teaspoon salt
Generous grating of
  pepper
1 tablespoon curry
  powder
2 cans beef OR
  mushroom gravy

Preheat the broiler. Line the broiler pan or other shallow pan with heavy duty foil. Place the lamb, onions and celery in it. Brush them with the steak sauce and place under broiler. Brown lightly, tossing so second side browns. Turn off the broiler and set thermostat for 325°F. Remove pan, add apple, sprinkle with the seasonings and pour the gravy over. Cover food with a second piece of foil and seal tightly. Place in the oven and bake for 1½ hours. Two tablespoons of dairy sour cream may be stirred into the sauce just before serving, if desired.
Great go-with: Buttered rice, chutney or sweet mixed pickles.

BROILER PAN GOULASH   *(6 servings)*

2 pounds beef round,
  cut in 1-inch cubes
2 cups chopped onions
4 tablespoons melted
  butter
2 tablespoons bottled
  steak sauce

2 teaspoons salt
2 teaspoons paprika
1 1-pound can tomato
  purée
2 tablespoons
  instant blending flour
½ cup chopped parsley

Trim excess fat from meat. Preheat broiler. Line broiler pan or other shallow pan with heavy duty foil; place meat and onions in it. Brush them with butter and steak sauce; brown lightly under the broiler, tossing so that second side also browns. Reset thermostat to 325°F and remove pan. Add seasonings and purée, into which the flour has been stirred. Cover with a second piece of foil, seal edges tightly. Place in the oven; bake for 2 hours. Serve thickly sprinkled with parsley.

CHICKEN IN PACKAGES

Chicken parts with vegetables and flavorings may be cooked together in individual foil packages. These packaged dinners are delectably flavored, the chicken moist and tender. Serve the packages right at the table, letting each person open his own to savor the aroma and enjoy the novelty.

A 2-pound broiler-fryer chicken, cut up, serves 3 people. Neck, giblets, back pieces may be saved for soup. Here are preparation steps:

1. Remove sharp protruding bones that may puncture foil.
2. Brown chicken and vegetables lightly.
3. Tear 3 squares of Heavy Duty Reynolds Wrap about 14 x 18 inches.
4. Arrange chicken, vegetables, other ingredients in center of foil square, dividing equally.
5. Seal foil, place packages on shallow pan and bake in 375°F oven for about 50 minutes.

GOOD CHICKEN-PACKAGE COMBINATIONS

Lemon Barbecued Chicken: Brown chicken lightly in butter; arrange on foil. In same skillet, brown 3 tablespoons chopped onion; sprinkle over chicken. Season each serving with 1 tablespoon brown sugar, ¼ teaspoon mustard, ¼ teaspoon salt and pepper. Rinse skillet with 3 tablespoons lemon juice and pour over chicken. Seal and bake as above.

Spanish Chicken: Brown chicken in olive oil, then arrange on 3 squares of heavy duty foil. Allow 2 small white onions and half a green pepper, cut in large dice, for each serving—brown these lightly in same skillet. Arrange over chicken. Season with a small piece of garlic crushed in 1 teaspoon salt and freshly ground pepper. Spoon over 1 8-ounce can tomato sauce with mushrooms dividing it equally. Seal packages and bake as above.

Tropical Chicken: Brown chicken lightly in butter and arrange on 3 squares of heavy duty foil. In same skillet, brown 3 slices of pineapple, well drained, and ½ cup slivered almonds or whole macadamia nuts, and arrange over chicken. Sprinkle each serving with salt, pepper and just a little rosemary and tarragon—either fresh or dried. Seal package and bake as above.

136

BAKED CHICKEN AND MUSHROOMS (*4 servings*)

*2 chicken breasts, split
    in half
4 tablespoons butter
½ pound fresh
    mushrooms, sliced* OR
1 6-ounce can, drained

*½ teaspoon rosemary
¾ teaspoon salt
Generous grating of
    pepper
4 tablespoons flour
1 pint light cream*

Brown chicken breasts very lightly in the butter, using an aluminum skillet. Have ready 4 pieces of heavy duty foil 12 x 18 inches. Place a chicken breast in center of each. Sauté mushrooms quickly in same skillet and add to each serving and season with rosemary, salt, pepper.

Add flour to butter remaining in skillet. Stir and cook 2 minutes. Add cream, stir and cook until sauce is thickened. Add ½ teaspoon salt, a sprinkling of pepper.

Pour over chicken breasts, dividing equally. Bring long ends of foil up over chicken breasts; overlap 1 or 2 inches. Close other ends by turning up to hold juices. Place packages on shallow pan; bake in 350°F oven 1 hour. To serve, place each package on serving plate. *Short-cut way:* Substitute 1 can condensed chicken, celery or mushroom soup and ¼ cup light cream for the sauce. Reduce the salt to ¼ teaspoon.

Great go-withs: Delectable with buttered rice and a mixed green salad.

CHICKEN EUGENIE (*6 servings*)

*2 center slices
    ready-to-eat ham
    (¼ inch thick)
4 tablespoons butter or
    margarine
3 chicken breasts, split
    in half*

*Salt and pepper
2 stalks celery, finely
    chopped
1 teaspoon minced onion
½ cup cream or top milk
1 can condensed cream
    of chicken soup*

Cut ham in 6 serving portions. Sauté until lightly browned on both sides in 1 tablespoon of the butter. Place each portion on 12 x 18 inch piece of heavy duty foil. In the same frying pan, lightly sauté chicken breasts in remaining butter. Place 1 on each ham serving. Sprinkle very lightly with salt and pepper. Add the celery, onion, and cream to the cream of chicken soup. Pour ½ cup over

137

each portion of ham and chicken. Close the foil by overlapping over chicken and folding ends up so there will be no danger of juices leaking. Place packages on shallow pan and bake in 350°F oven 1 hour. Place packages on serving plates; open and fold back foil.

Good to know: This is a good party recipe. If guests don't arrive on time, the packages can stand in oven, heat turned off, and no harm will be done. They stay hot and the flavor improves.

CHICKEN AND VEGETABLES IN A BUNDLE *(4 servings)*

1 2½-pound broiler-fryer, cut in quarters
8 very small onions
1 large Idaho potato, quartered
4 small tender carrots, sliced or julienne
Generous grating of pepper
¼ teaspoon salt
Generous sprinkling of paprika
4 pinches of packaged herbs for salads
1 can condensed cream of chicken soup

Rinse chicken and pat dry. Have ready 4 large squares of heavy duty foil. Place a chicken quarter on each. Add vegetables, dividing equally. Season each serving. Pour chicken soup over, dividing it equally. Close foil; place packages on pan. Bake in 375°F oven 1 hour.

HINTS FOR THE INSTANT GOURMET COOK

If most of your cooking must be done without lengthy preparation, keep products such as these on hand to add special touches that will raise your meals to new heights:

Dehydrated gravy and sauce mixes and canned gravies, for making gravies and sauces quickly. Use them in casserole dishes too.

Frozen and canned vegetables, canned tomatoes, and tomato sauces. Include some of the more unusual items such as artichoke hearts, snow peas, the new vegetable combinations with sauce, Chinese water chestnuts, marrons.

Canned soups and dry soup mixes, good both for serving as soup and for use as sauces and gravies.

Frozen or freeze-dried chives and parsley, either your own freezing or in little plastic jars from the supermarket.

Nuts, both whole and in broken bits. Almonds, particularly the already slivered almonds, are so useful for adding crunchiness to many main dishes and desserts.

Pimento, both whole or in pieces for adding flavor and color to main dishes and salads.

Gelatins, packaged puddings, all to be given your own quick, individual touch.

Cooking wines, a bottle of vermouth and one of sherry—the first for most meat and fish dishes, the second for desserts as well as main dishes.

Bottled steak sauce and Kitchen Bouquet, to add color, help to brown meats, and add zesty flavor.

Instant blending flour for thickening gravies and sauces quickly and to do away with sifting flour for its many uses.

Freeze-dried, canned and frozen mushrooms for quick adding to casseroles, sauces and many dishes.

Cheese already grated. Parmesan and other types of cheese are available in shaker jars and cannisters for topping appetizers and casseroles, and for adding to sauces.

Herbs, dehydrated and packaged in jars. These are available in blends for use in salads, and in fish, poultry and meat dishes.

Onion and garlic in flake and powder form or as flavored salt.

Seasoned salt and pepper. Often these add needed zip to dishes.

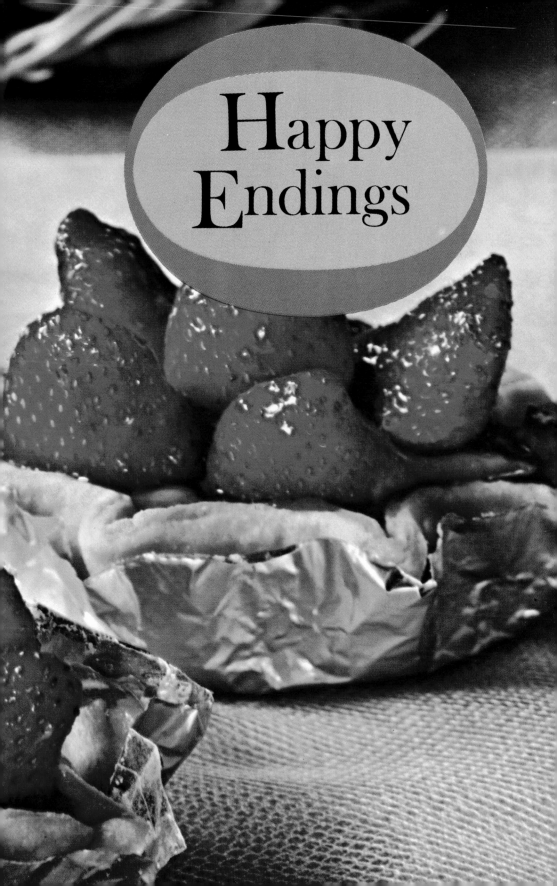

Happy Endings

Happy Endings

Wrap your imagination in foil and turn out specialty-of-the-house desserts. Try some of these, for a start

For many, dessert is the best part of the meal—and for almost everyone, no meal is quite complete without a sweet ending. Much as many of us wish we could eliminate the calories, dessert is something we all enjoy. Reynolds Wrap can do a lot to help with the preparation of desserts. Here are some of our favorite recipes, which are easier and more fun to make when Reynolds Wrap is used.

SPICY BAKED APPLES IN FOIL

For truly handsome and fine-tasting baked apples, good baking apples are a necessity. Rome Beauties are our preference. Remove the cores and peel halfway down from stem end. Place each apple on a large square of foil. Fill centers with sugar, cinnamon, nutmeg, a generous dot of butter. Or fill with raisins, nutmeats, and a small amount of sugar. Bring foil up over apples and crumple ends together, but not tightly. Some steam should escape. Place wrapped apples on a shallow pan and bake at 375°F 45 minutes. Turn back foil about 10 minutes before apples are expected to be done. Test by piercing with fork. Spoon juices in foil over apples and continue baking. Serve warm or cold with cream.

BANANAS FLAMBÉE

Select bananas that are ripe, but firm. Peel and split lengthwise. Place a sheet of foil on a shallow pan; arrange the bananas on it. Turn up edges of foil to hold juice. Brush bananas with melted butter or margarine and sprinkle with sugar and cinnamon. Place under broiler until just tinged with brown, basting with a little more butter while broiling. Remove, foil and all, to a hot serving plate. Warm 2 tablespoons of dark rum for each serving and pour over the bananas. Light the rum and spoon it over the bananas as it burns. Serve with vanilla ice cream or whipped cream.

In color picture: Strawberry Party Tarts

GREEN GRAPES WITH COINTREAU

1 pound seedless green grapes	*¼ cup light brown sugar*
	¼ cup cinnamon
1 pint dairy sour cream	*Cointreau*

This is the "what is it" dessert, delicious and so easy to prepare! Wash and remove stems from grapes. Drain thoroughly, then fold into the sour cream. Cover bowl with foil and refrigerate for one hour or until thoroughly chilled. Serve in sherbet glasses. Pass attractive small dishes, one with brown sugar, one with cinnamon, and a small decanter of Cointreau. Each person seasons his own dessert, sprinkling on the brown sugar and cinnamon and pouring on a little of the liqueur. Pass the condiments a second time as, after the first taste, more of the condiments may make this dessert taste even better.

This is a delightful dessert for a Hawaiian luau or a party with a Caribbean theme. It can be prepared well ahead and brought from the freezer, as the handsome, perfect finishing touch at the end of an exotic dinner.

FROZEN PINEAPPLE

Select very small pineapples and let them ripen one or two days if necessary. Cut them in half lengthwise right through the green top, leaving the tops on. Cut out the cores, then loosen and remove the fruit, leaving a firm shell. Dice the fruit and combine with 2 tablespoons each of sugar and rum for each cup of diced pineapple. Refill the shells not quite full; cover with foil and place in the freezer for 1 hour or until very thoroughly chilled. Remove and top each filled pineapple half with vanilla or any fruit-flavored ice cream or sherbet. Sprinkle with coconut. Wrap completely with foil and store in the freezer. They may be kept for 24 hours. The pineapple should only partially freeze—the sugar and rum keep it from getting too hard.

STEAMED PUDDINGS

Steamed puddings are wonderful old fashioned desserts that deserve a revival of popularity. They may be made ahead and stored in the refrigerator for a few days—or for many months in the freezer. Use custard cups, small bowls or aluminum cans for individual servings—a larger bowl for pudding to serve many. Fill each bowl only ⅔ full so pudding has plenty of room to rise.

The small aluminum cans used for potted meats, some brands of dehydrated soups and tuna are seamless on the bottom and sides. These make fine individual molds. Puddings slip out easily. Heavy Duty Reynolds Wrap makes a good cover that will fit any container.
How to steam puddings: Use any pan large enough to accommodate the individual or large pudding. Put a wire rack in the bottom of the pan and place puddings on the rack. Pour in boiling water until it comes halfway up the sides of pudding containers. Cover pan and boil gently. Use towel to protect fingers when removing the finished pudding.
How to freeze: If you don't need the containers for reuse, simply cool, seal foil cover and freeze. Or cool and turn out puddings, package in heavy duty foil wrap and freeze.
Pressure-cooked puddings: Follow directions in instruction booklet that came with the cooker. It will reduce the cooking time. Secure foil cover on mold by tying with string.
To serve steamed puddings: Reheat in the oven, still sealed in foil. If puddings are chilled, reheat individual puddings 45 minutes at 300°F, a large pudding 1½ hours at 300°F. If puddings are frozen, allow 10 minutes additional time.
To serve Flaming Plum Pudding: Heat ½ cup brandy or rum in a small pan until lukewarm. Pour over large pudding or several small puddings arranged on warm serving plate. Light with match and bring to table. Spoon flaming liquor quickly over puddings. Or moisten lumps of sugar in lemon or orange extract and arrange around pudding, or place one lump on top of each individual pudding. Light lumps with match.

HOLIDAY STEAMED FIG PUDDING (8 servings)

½ pound dried figs	¼ pound kidney suet,
1 cup milk	chopped
1½ cups sifted flour	¾ cup sugar
1½ teaspoons baking	2 eggs, beaten
powder	1 cup dry bread crumbs
1 teaspoon nutmeg	2 teaspoons grated
½ teaspoon salt	orange rind

Stem figs and cut in pieces. Combine with milk; cook, covered, in double boiler about 20 minutes. Cool to lukewarm. Sift dry ingredients together. Place suet and sugar in a bowl; work together, using the hands or electric beater. Add eggs and beat until blended. Add dry bread crumbs, orange rind, and the dry ingredients alternately with the milk and figs. Beat until blended. Turn into several small containers or one large, buttered. Boil individual puddings gently 50 minutes, large pudding 2 hours. Serve hot with Hard Sauce or Velvet Sauce.

STEAMED CHOCOLATE PUDDING *(8 servings)*

2 cups sifted flour
2 teaspoons baking
   powder
¼ teaspoon salt
3 tablespoons butter or
   margarine

⅔ cup sugar
1 egg
1 cup milk
2 squares unsweetened
   chocolate, melted
1 teaspoon vanilla

Sift dry ingredients together. Cream butter and sugar, then add the egg and beat until light. Add the dry ingredients alternately with the milk, mixing well. Fold in the chocolate and the vanilla. Fill buttered individual cups or small cans or a 1-quart bowl. Cover with foil and steam individual puddings 40 minutes, large puddings about 1½ hours. Serve hot with Velvet Sauce.

VELVET SAUCE *(8 servings)*

2 eggs
1 cup confectioners'
   sugar
3 tablespoons lemon
   juice

3 tablespoons brandy,
   rum, OR
1 teaspoon vanilla
½ pint heavy cream,
   whipped

Beat the eggs. Add sugar gradually, then the lemon juice and the flavoring, continuing to beat until mixture is very light and fluffy. Fold in the whipped cream. Refrigerate until ready to serve. This is good on hot steamed puddings and on hot dessert soufflés.

HARD SAUCE *(10 servings)*

½ cup butter or
   margarine
1 cup confectioners'
   sugar

1 teaspoon brandy,
   rum OR
1 teaspoon vanilla
Nutmeg

Have the butter at room temperature. Beat it with the sugar until very light and fluffy. Add flavoring. Spoon into foil pie plate or pan, spread out, sprinkle with nutmeg; cover with foil. Chill until firm; cut into squares. Can be stored in the refrigerator tightly covered for 1 week. For longer storage, freeze. Top hot desserts with a square of sauce.

Hard Sauce Rosettes: Place mixture in a pastry bag. Force out onto a sheet of foil; chill or freeze until firm. Cover with foil.

Fluffy Light Hard Sauce: Add ½ cup heavy cream, beating until the sauce is very light. Spoon onto hot desserts.

SPRING FORM OR CHEESECAKE PAN

Stores are filled with a wonderful array of fine aluminum pans these days and it is nearly always possible to get just the right shape and size pan needed for a particular recipe.

But very special pans such as spring form pans and soufflé dishes are not always readily obtainable. They can be made from Heavy Duty Reynolds Wrap and will last through one or more uses.

Spring Form Pan: Trace a circle the desired size on lightweight cardboard. (Shirt cardboard is fine.) Spring form pans usually come in 6, 8 and 10 inch diameters. Cover the circle with foil, securing it on the bottom with tape. Multiply the diameter by 4 and tear off a length of heavy duty foil to correspond. Fold this foil in half lengthwise and in half again to make a band 4½ inches wide. Cut short ½-inch snips on one long side at 1-inch intervals. Place the foil-covered circle on a can or other object to elevate it. Fold the foil band around it, attaching it by bending the snipped ends flat against the bottom of the circle. Attach these with tape. Let the band overlap and secure it with tape. Stand upright and fill with food. Place on a shallow pan if the foil pan contains food which is to be baked.

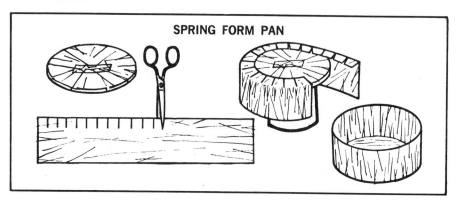

SPRING FORM PAN

Here is a luscious dessert, sinfully rich and fattening. Serve it when you throw all caution to the winds. It may be made a day or more ahead and looks very beautiful unmolded and garnished with whipped cream, maraschino cherries, or pistachio nuts.

CHOCOLATE REFRIGERATOR CAKE   *(6 servings)*

3 squares unsweetened
  chocolate
6 tablespoons
  granulated sugar
3 tablespoons milk
3 eggs, separated
1 teaspoon vanilla
⅛ teaspoon salt
¾ cup unsalted butter

¾ cup confectioners'
  sugar
1½ dozen ladyfingers
¼ cup brandy and ¼
  cup water, mixed
½ cup whipped cream,
Pistachio nuts,
  cherries

Melt the chocolate with sugar and milk in top of double boiler. Add the beaten egg yolks; cook, stirring, until smooth and thick. Cool, add the vanilla and salt. Cream the butter and ½ cup of confectioners' sugar and fold into the chocolate mixture. Fold in the egg whites beaten with the remaining confectioners' sugar. Line a small loaf pan with foil, or make a 6-inch spring form pan (page 146). Dip the ladyfingers in the brandy mixture and arrange them in the bottom and around the sides of the pan. You will have to break off small pieces of the ladyfingers in order to have them the right size. Spoon in a layer of the chocolate mixture, add the broken lady fingers and cover with remaining chocolate mixture. Top with more lady fingers. Cover with foil and chill in the refrigerator overnight. To serve, if molded in loaf pan, grasp foil liner and loosen the dessert, then invert on a serving plate. Remove foil. If molded in spring form pan, remove sides, invert and remove foil base. Garnish with whipped cream, cherries and/or pistachio nuts.

Good to know: When preparing molded desserts, think ahead to serving them. A beautiful round dessert should have a round dish, a loaf-shaped dessert an oval or rectangular dish.

This cheesecake is rich, but not cloyingly so. It is our favorite of many recipes we have tested.

FAVORITE CHEESECAKE   *(12 servings)*

1 6-ounce package zwieback	*1 8-ounce package cream cheese*
½ cup confectioners' sugar	*4 eggs*
½ cup butter or margarine, melted	*1 cup sugar*
1 pint creamed cottage cheese	*½ teaspoon salt*
	Grated rind and juice of 1 large lemon
	½ pint heavy cream

Roll the zwieback on a board with rolling pin or put in a blender to make crumbs. Combine with sugar, then add the butter or margarine and stir to combine. Pat a layer of crumbs into the bottom of a round 8 x 3 inch spring form pan (page 146), spreading them up the sides as far as possible. Save ½ cup crumbs for top of cake.

Place cottage cheese in bowl of electric mixer and beat to remove any lumps. Add cream cheese, continuing to beat, then the eggs and all remaining ingredients. Blend thoroughly and pour into the crumb-lined pan. Top with the ½ cup crumbs. Bake at 250°F about 2 hours, or until cake is firm to the touch. A silver knife inserted should come out clean. Cool where cake will not be in a draft. Remove sides of pan, transfer base with cake to serving plate.

Meringues are delightful desserts, easy to prepare with an electric mixer or beater, tasty and pretty for party occasions. They may be baked on foil, from which they can be removed very easily. They should not brown during baking—rather just turn the palest of champagne colors. One word of warning—don't make them in very humid weather. To be at their best, meringue shells and layers should be crisp, to contrast with the fillings. Meringues can be made ahead and stored in a cool place. Place them on a foil pie plate or pan, cover and seal tightly with foil. Don't refrigerate, except for short periods, and don't freeze.

MERINGUES GLACEES   *(6 to 8 servings)*

3 egg whites	*½ teaspoon vanilla*
⅛ teaspoon salt	*Vanilla, chocolate or strawberry ice cream*
1 cup granulated sugar	
½ teaspoon lemon juice OR *vinegar*	

Have egg whites at room temperature. Add the salt to them and beat with an electric mixer or hand beater until soft peaks can be formed. Start adding the sugar gradually and beat continuously until all the sugar has been added and the meringue is very stiff. Add the lemon juice or vinegar and vanilla, beating it in at the last. Drop by high, rounded, large spoonfuls on a cookie sheet lined with foil—no need to grease. Bake at 250°F 1 hour. Remove to a cake rack and cool. To serve, split meringues in half, place a large spoonful of ice cream on lower half and cover with top. Serve with chocolate or fruit sauce.

Meringue Kisses: Fold ⅔ cup chopped walnuts or other nuts into meringue mixture. Bake as above. Serve as a cookie.

LEMON DELIGHT MERINGUES   *(6 servings)*

Prepare the meringues as above. Drop by spoonfuls about 3 inches in diameter on foil-covered cookie sheet. Make a 2-inch hollow in the center of each, shaping the sides up high. Bake at 250°F 1 hour. Remove to wire rack and cool. Fill with the following: In top of double boiler, combine 3 egg yolks with ¼ cup sugar, 4 tablespoons lemon juice, 1½ teaspoons grated lemon rind. Beat just enough to blend. Cook over boiling water until thick. Cool and chill. Fold into ½ pint heavy cream, whipped. Chill the filling. Fill the meringue nests before serving, and chill again for 30 minutes. This filling is also delicious when prepared with fresh limes.

For a bridal shower, try this decorative idea: Make silver scalloped holders and little umbrellas for meringues as follows: Cut 6-inch squares of foil. Fold in half; then in quarters. Then fold from the closed corner diagonally 3 times. With scissors, cut the wide end in a scallop. Open out to a scalloped circle. Place circles on dessert plate under meringues. Turn up scalloped edges all around. Umbrellas: Make the same way, using cocktail pick to hold them over dessert.

Cream puffs are a most versatile and delightful dessert. They may be made large or small; the dough may be shaped into éclairs and other forms, and they all may be filled in a variety of ways. Excellent cream puff mixes are available in markets, but making the dough from scratch is easy and fun. Baked cream puffs freeze beautifully and may be kept for 6 to 8 weeks.

CREAM PUFFS   *(12 to 14 large puffs)*

1 cup water	*1 cup flour*
¼ pound butter or	*¼ teaspoon salt*
margarine	*4 eggs*

Place the water and butter in a saucepan; heat until the butter is melted. Reduce the heat to low and add the flour and salt all at once. Using a wooden spoon, stir and beat until mixture leaves sides of pan and forms a smooth ball. Remove from heat; add the unbeaten eggs, one at a time, stirring vigorously after each. The mixture should be very thick, smooth and shiny when all eggs have been added. Line a cookie sheet with foil and drop the dough by tablespoons, 2 inches apart, rounding each spoonful up as high as possible. Bake at 400°F about 50 minutes. Cool on a wire rack. Make a slit on one side and fill with ice cream or custard filling. Dust with confectioners' sugar or serve with chocolate sauce.

Profiteroles: These are simply tiny cream puffs. Drop cream puff dough by rounded teaspoonfuls onto foil-covered cookie sheet and bake at 400°F about 30 minutes. Fill with ice cream or custard filling. These tiny puffs look dainty and delicious served 3 or more on a pretty dessert plate with a sauce poured over. The above recipe makes about 40 tiny puffs.

Éclairs: Put cream puff dough through a pastry bag, using large round ¾-inch tube. Form a roll about 3 inches long, ¾ inch thick. Or drop from tablespoon, elongating dough to this shape. Bake at 400°F 45 minutes. Fill as for cream puffs, frost as desired.

Paris Brest: Place foil on a cookie sheet and mark an 8-inch circle on it. With a pastry bag or spoon form dough into a wreath, having it about 1½ inches wide and as high as possible. Sprinkle top with slivered blanched almonds, pressing them in. Bake at 400°F 15 minutes, reduce heat to 350°F and continue baking about 40 minutes longer. Cool on cake rack. Split the ring and fill with whipped cream or custard filling; garnish with whipped cream, grated chocolate and toasted slivered almonds. To serve, cut in slices.

Freezing Cream Puffs: Cream puffs, particularly the little ones, are a wonderful dessert to have on hand in the freezer. Split them, fill with ice cream and put them in the freezer until firm. Arrange on foil-covered cardboard, completely wrap in foil, label, and return to the freezer. Large cream puffs and éclairs may be handled in the same way. Ice cream is the best filling if you wish the dessert ready. Serve the frozen puffs with a hot chocolate or other hot sauce. The puffs without filling may be frozen in the same way. To serve, place them in a 325°F oven 10 minutes to regain crispness, then fill. The large Paris Brest may be frozen if an ice cream filling is used. Garnish it with whipped cream and almonds.

DELICIOUS AND EASY WAYS WITH PASTRY DESSERTS

Everyone enjoys pies and pastry desserts, but they take time to prepare. Here is an easy way to serve these good things to your family frequently and to have delightful pastry desserts on hand.

Make pastry ahead of time. Roll out into circles, ready for shaping, or fit into plates ready for filling, or shape into individual tarts. Package these pastries in Heavy Duty Reynolds Wrap and freeze. They will keep for as long as 3 months and will be ready for fruit or other seasonal fillings at a moment's notice, since they do not need thawing.

Some filled pies may be frozen; a list is given. It is generally better to freeze unbaked pastries and bake when needed. If they are frozen *after* baking, they need to be put in the oven for freshening, and thawing a baked pie takes almost as much time as baking a frozen one. Here are directions for preparing pastry and procedures for freezing.

STANDARD PASTRY

(3 2-crust 9-inch pies OR *6 11-inch circles* OR
18 4½-inch circles for tarts)

6 cups sifted all-purpose flour	*2 cups shortening (part butter or margarine)*
3 teaspoons salt	*¾ cup cold water (about)*

Sift flour and salt together into a large mixing bowl. Add the shortening and cut in with 2 knives or pastry blender. Sprinkle with the water, mixing with a fork until all the mixture is moistened. Gather the dough together in small amounts and press with the hands to form into 6 balls about 3 inches in diameter. Flatten balls slightly, place them on a piece of foil, cover and place in the refrigerator. Remove one at a time for rolling.

Pastry circles: Roll out pie dough ⅛ inch in thickness. Using pie plate as a guide, cut circles, allowing extra for forming fluted crust or for turning under. Cut a circle from cardboard, slightly larger than pastry, and cover with foil. Stack pastry circles on this, separating them with foil circles so they won't stick. Place in the freezer until firm, then overwrap with heavy duty foil, label, and return to freezer. Circles may be removed in the number needed. They take only 5 minutes to soften, and may be used for bottom or top crusts. An 11-inch circle fits a 9-inch pie plate.

Pastry shells: Use foil or other inexpensive pie plates. Roll out pastry and fit into these plates, forming a crimped or other decorative rim. Place in freezer until firm, then nest one on top of the other and overwrap with heavy duty foil. Label and return to freezer. If these are to be filled after baking, prick with fork when taken from freezer and bake at 450°F, allowing 25 minutes.

Filled 2-crust pies: Rhubarb, blueberry, cherry, mince, prune, cranberry and raisin pies may be completely made ready for the oven and will freeze perfectly. Apple, peach, fresh apricot or other fruits which darken when peeled and cut should be sprinkled with a vitamin C preparation, Fruit Fresh, sold at food and drug stores.

To freeze filled pies, place them in the freezer until firm; wrap in heavy duty foil, label, return to freezer.

To bake frozen pies, cut slits in the top crust, if not already cut. They should not be thawed. They will take 15 to 20 minutes longer than unfrozen pies to bake. Bake at 450°F for 20 minutes; reduce temperature to 350°F and continue baking 30 to 40 minutes.

The bottom crust of frozen pies is sometimes difficult to brown. Spreading the bottom of the pie plate with butter or margarine before placing crust in it and baking the pie on a lower shelf in the oven helps overcome this difficulty.

FRESH BLUEBERRY PIE   *(8 servings)*

*2 11-inch circles to fit
    a 9-inch pie plate*
*4 cups or 1 quart fresh
    blueberries*
¾ cup sugar
2 tablespoons flour OR

*1½ tablespoons
    quick-cooking tapioca*
Sprinkling of nutmeg
*1 tablespoon butter or
    margarine*

Fit a pastry circle into pie plate. Rinse berries, drain them well, then turn them out on a soft towel, to remove all possible water. Place about half of them in the pastry. Combine sugar, flour or tapioca, and nutmeg. Sprinkle about half over berries. Add remaining berries, and sugar mixture. Top with dots of butter. Brush edge of pastry with water. Fold second pastry circle and cut slits along fold in center. Place over berries, opening out. Seal to bottom crust by turning under. Press with fork or the end of a spoon to form decorative edging. Bake at 450°F 12 to 15 minutes, then reduce heat to 350°F and bake 15 minutes longer.

Bright pink hothouse rhubarb is a harbinger of Spring that appears soon after the first of the year. It makes a delicately flavored and beautiful pie. Garden rhubarb has a somewhat more forthright flavor and is also delicious. Don't dream of peeling rhubarb—simply remove discolorations and trim off stem ends.

SPRING RHUBARB PIE   *(8 servings)*

1 11-inch pastry circle
1½ pounds rhubarb, cut
  in ¾-inch pieces
1½ cups granulated
  sugar
4 tablespoons flour
½ teaspoon grated
  nutmeg

1 egg, slightly beaten
TOPPING:
½ cup sugar
⅓ cup flour
¼ cup butter or
  margarine

Fit pastry circle into 9-inch pie plate; turn overhang under, and with fingers flute edge to make a high stand-up rim. Place rhubarb in bowl and toss with the sugar, flour, nutmeg and egg. Turn into the pastry-lined plate. Blend last 3 ingredients together to form a crumbly topping. Spread over pie evenly. Bake in 425°F oven 20 minutes, then reduce heat to 350°F and continue baking 20 minutes or until rhubarb can be pierced with a fork.

TIPS FOR PIE BAKERS

To make a perfect top: For a lovely, shiny top crust, brush with cream, or 1 egg yolk beaten with 3 tablespoons of light cream. Brush with melted butter or margarine if top crust does not brown as well as it should. If top crust or tops of open pies brown too rapidly, cover loosely with foil.

To keep outer edge of pie from burning: Tear off 1½-inch-wide strips of standard foil; join 3 strips together to make strip 35 inches long, for a 9-inch pie. Crease through center lengthwise. Place around rim of pie before putting pie in oven. If crust is very delicate, chill in refrigerator a few minutes before placing foil on rim. Remove the foil after pie has baked for 15 minutes.

To protect the oven from runovers: Most fruit pies—particularly double-crust ones—have a tendency to run over. Don't fill too full with fruit. If runovers seem likely, place a piece of foil, slightly larger than the pie all around, on the shelf below the one on which pie rests. Turn up edges a little to hold juice. Don't use too large a piece as this interferes with browning the bottom of pie. Don't place it under pie until juice looks likely to run out. If there is a lot of juice that has run out, it can be poured back in after pie has finished baking.

To store pies: Pies are at their delicious best as soon after baking as it's possible to serve them. Leftovers may be stored at room temperature, if filled with fruit. Cream-filled pies and others that spoil easily should be covered with foil, stored in the refrigerator.

TART SHELLS MADE WITH REYNOLDS WRAP

Tart shells for attractive desserts, chicken à la king, and other good things, are easily made with the help of Reynolds Wrap. There's no need for special pans, and they may be made any size and shape to fit party occasions.

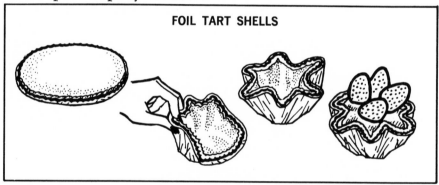

FOIL TART SHELLS

1. Using a saucer as a guide, cut circles of Heavy Duty Reynolds Wrap. A circle of 4½-inch diameter will make a 2½-inch tart.
2. Cut matching circles of pastry rolled ⅛ inch thick.
3. Place pastry circles on top of foil circles. Prick all over with a fork if they are to be baked without filling, otherwise don't prick. (At this point, circles may be frozen.)
4. With thumb and forefinger, turn up edge of foil and pastry together 1 inch all around; pinch at 1-inch intervals, to hold edge up.
5. Place on shallow pan or cookie sheet and bake unfilled tarts at 450°F 15 minutes, or until delicately brown. Follow individual recipes for tarts baked with fillings.

Square tarts: Using a ruler, cut foil into 5-inch squares. Roll pastry; using ruler, cut pastry into matching squares. Place pastry squares on foil squares; turn up edges 1 inch all around and pinch at corners to hold firm.

Party tarts: Cut pattern from shirt cardboard in form of heart, star, bell, or other shape suited to the occasion. Cut foil and pastry, turn up edges and pinch.

Freezing tart shells: Arrange on foil-covered cardboard and place in freezer until firm. Overwrap in foil, label, and return to freezer. Tart shells filled with pecan filling (page 156) may be baked before freezing. Since they are small they defrost quickly and are restored to crispness by heating in the oven 20 minutes at 300°F.

STRAWBERRY PARTY TARTS *(18 servings)*

18 baked tart shells
2 packages vanilla pudding
½ pint heavy cream, whipped
3 pints fresh strawberries
1 8-ounce glass red currant jelly
4 tablespoons water

Cool the tart shells thoroughly. Prepare the pudding according to package directions; chill if necessary. Fold in the whipped cream. Place a spoonful of mixture in each tart shell. Top with strawberries, piling them up as high as possible. Melt currant jelly with the water. When completely melted and smooth, spoon over the berries, coating them to give them a lovely shiny look. Chill for at least 1 hour before serving.

Cracker and cookie crumb crusts are easy to prepare and delicious. Here is a frozen chiffon pie made with graham cracker crust. It is served frozen, but is best when taken from the freezer and refrigerated for 1 or 2 hours before serving. The recipe makes 2 pies, which can be kept 6 or 7 weeks in the freezer.

FROZEN LIME PIE *(16 servings)*

Crust:
24 graham crackers
¾ cup pecans
⅓ cup sugar
⅔ cup melted butter or margarine
½ teaspoon cinnamon

Put crackers and nuts through food chopper or blender, or crush and chop with rolling pin and knife. Toss with the remaining ingredients. Butter 2 10-inch pie pans; pat mixture on bottom and sides. Reserve ½ cup to sprinkle on top. Bake crusts at 325°F 10 minutes. Cool.

Filling:
6 eggs, separated
1 cup sugar
⅛ teaspoon salt
2 tablespoons grated
　lime rind

½ cup fresh lime juice
1 pint heavy cream,
　whipped

Place egg yolks in top of double boiler. Add ½ cup of the sugar, salt, lime rind and juice. Beat until blended, then cook over hot water until mixture coats a spoon and is thickened and smooth. Chill thoroughly. Fold in cream and egg whites stiffly beaten with remaining sugar. Pour into cooled crusts. Sprinkle with remaining crumbs and place in freezer until firm. If not served immediately, cover with foil, sealing tightly.

Graham cracker, chocolate cookie and frozen pastry crusts already shaped and in foil pie plates are available in food markets. Keep them on hand on the supply shelf and in the freezer. These convenient crusts make it very easy to serve a fine home-baked pie. Here is a quick filling that everyone finds delectable.

JEAN KLEVER'S QUICK PECAN PIE　　　*(8 to 10 servings)*

1 9-inch frozen, unbaked
　pastry shell
3 eggs
¼ cup butter, melted

2 cups dark brown sugar
¼ cup milk
1 teaspoon vanilla
¾ to 1 cup pecans

Remove pastry shell from freezer. Break eggs into a bowl, add melted butter, sugar, milk and vanilla. Beat with electric mixer or spoon until well combined. Add pecans. Pour into shell. Bake in 325°F oven for 50 minutes. Cool and serve topped with a little slightly-sweetened whipped cream.

Europeans seldom serve pies as we know them. The English make flans, the French make tarts. Both are pastry shells, either round or rectangular, filled with beautifully arranged fruit and other ingredients. They do not have top crusts. Both call for the use of a flan ring.

The flan ring makes it possible to serve such a dessert on an elegant plate or serving dish without the pan in which it was baked. Flan rings can be found in this country, in very special shops—but how much easier to make one on the spot, from Heavy Duty Reynolds Wrap!

REYNOLDS WRAP FLAN RING

For a 10-inch flan ring, tear off 3⅓ feet of heavy duty foil. Spread it out on a long table and fold double lengthwise, then over and over until you have a band about 1¼ inches wide. Form this into a circle with a 10-inch diameter, joining the band with a paper clip or straight pin. Or form into a rectangle of the desired size.

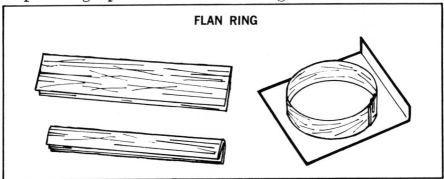

FLAN RING

To use the flan ring, place it on a cookie sheet or other flat pan without sides. Fit the pastry into the ring, trimming it at the top or making a decorative edge. It may be baked with or without filling. When pastry is baked, unfasten foil band and remove. Slide flan or tart onto serving plate.

ROSY PEAR FLAN *(8 to 10 servings)*

*1 11-inch pastry circle
(page 151)* OR
*Pastry made from 1½
cups flour*
*3 tablespoons finely
chopped almonds*
*3 tablespoons soft stale
bread crumbs*
4 fresh Bartlett pears

⅓ cup granulated sugar
*⅓ cup brown sugar,
packed*
⅛ teaspoon salt
1 tablespoon butter
½ teaspoon cinnamon
¼ teaspoon nutmeg
⅓ cup tart red jelly

Line a 9-inch flan ring with pastry. Sprinkle the almonds and crumbs in the bottom. Peel, halve and core pears. Cut each half lengthwise into 4 slices. Combine sugars, salt, butter and spices with ½ cup water in a large skillet and bring to boil. Add pear slices and simmer, covered, 7 to 10 minutes, or until pears are slightly glazed. Remove slices from syrup and let cool. Boil syrup 3 to 5 minutes to thicken slightly. Cool. Arrange pear slices symmetrically in pastry, pour syrup over. Bake at 425°F 30 minutes. Melt the jelly and drizzle over the pears. Cool; remove foil flan ring. Slide onto serving plate. Serve with whipped cream.

CAKES AND COOKIES

Why anyone would want to make a cake or cookies from scratch these days with the multitude of mixes, refrigerated and frozen cakes and cookies available in markets would seem a question unanswerable. Yet there are a few of these delectable desserts that are so good that from time to time they seem worth the extra effort.

There are certain uses of Reynolds Wrap in cake making, whether a mix is used or not, that are basic. Here they are:

Sift flour and other dry ingredients onto a square of foil. Pick up foil, forming funnel shape at one corner, when adding ingredients to mixing bowl.

Measure out raisins, nuts, and other special ingredients on small pieces of foil.

Melt chocolate on a square of foil over warm setting on surface burner or in oven at 250°F.

Line pans with Reynolds Wrap. The 12-inch-wide standard Reynolds Wrap is fine for this purpose. If pan is square or rectangular, simply tear foil to fit over bottom and up 2 sides. If it is round, tear a square that will fit conveniently into the bottom of pan. Let one corner extend above edge of pan to use in releasing baked cake from pan. No need to grease the foil. A few drops of water sprinkled on the pan before placing foil in it will secure the foil and keep it from slipping. To line tube pans, use 2 or 3 narrow strips smoothed inside and extending above both outside and inner tube edge. Grease the pan. Tug on these strips to release cakes.

GOLDEN GLORY PICNIC CAKE

1 package yellow cake mix
1 29-ounce can cling peaches, drained
1 cup light brown sugar
¼ teaspoon nutmeg
1 cup slivered almonds
¼ cup melted butter or margarine
½ cup heavy cream

Line a 10 x 10 x 2 inch pan with heavy duty foil and butter it lightly. Prepare the cake mix, pour into the pan and bake according to package directions. Drain the peaches. When cake is just done, remove from oven and quickly arrange peaches over top. Sprinkle with the sugar, nutmeg and nuts. Pour over the melted butter or margarine, then the cream. Return to the oven for 10 minutes until topping is lightly browned. Take to picnic in pan, cut in squares to serve.

Skillet Cake: This cake may be baked in a large heavy weight aluminum skillet lined with foil. Try serving it warm with whipped cream.

TELL-YOUR-NEIGHBOR CAKE

> *1-pound 3-ounce*
> *package yellow cake*
> *mix*
> *1 3¾-ounce package*
> *lemon instant*
> *pudding*
>
> *1 cup water*
> *4 eggs*
> *Tinted coconut*
> *Silver dragées*
> *(optional)*

Combine cake mix, pudding mix, water, and eggs in large mixing bowl. Blend at low speed of electric mixer just to moisten. Then beat 8 minutes at medium speed. Line three 9-inch layer pans with foil. Pour batter into pans. Bake at 350°F 25 to 30 minutes, or until cake tester inserted into center comes out clean. Cool in pans 15 minutes; then remove from pans. Cool thoroughly on rack. Fill and frost with Beat 'n' Eat Frosting. Decorate cake with tinted coconut and silver dragées. Store uncovered in refrigerator.

Other ways: Use devil's food cake mix with one 3¾-ounce package banana cream or coconut cream instant pudding; or use white cake mix with one 4½-ounce package chocolate or chocolate fudge instant pudding.

Beat 'n' Eat Frosting: Combine 2 egg whites, 1½ cups sugar, ½ teaspoon cream of tartar, and 2 teaspoons vanilla in large mixing bowl; mix well. Add ½ cup boiling water and beat at high speed of electric mixer or with rotary beater until mixture will stand in stiff peaks—10 to 12 minutes.

Tinted coconut: Measure 2 tablespoons lime gelatin from package; combine with 1⅓ cups flaked coconut in a quart jar. Cover and shake vigorously until coconut is evenly tinted.

SHAPED PARTY CAKES

It's fun to bake cakes in shapes to suit the occasion—charming, familiar holiday symbols like a bunny or duck for Easter, a heart for Valentine's Day, a firecracker for Fourth of July, a black cat for Hallowe'en, or a snowman or Santa Claus for Christmas.

They can all be baked in pans you make yourself from Reynolds Wrap. All you need is the ability to draw a simple pattern freehand, or to trace one from an illustration. Forming the foil into a pan is easy. With these pans, use either a cake mix or your favorite recipe.

Here are directions for Easter Bunny Cake. This will give you the basic idea—then try your hand at other shapes.

EASTER BUNNY CAKE

Cut out bunny pattern and trace on thin cardboard, about 15 x 12 inches in size. (Shirt cardboards or tablet backs work fine—if too small, tape them together to give required size.) Cut out this shape, which will be the bottom of your baking pan; cover both sides with Heavy Duty Reynolds Wrap and tape into position on back.

For sides, cut 3 lengths of foil about 18 x 20 inches. Fold lengthwise in half, then fold the doubled length in half again, then a third time. This will give you 3 strips about 2 inches wide. On one long edge of each strip, snip in ½ inch at 1-inch intervals. Preform each strip to the edge of the foil-covered bunny outline, folding the ½-inch edge under the outline. Then fit each section on to the base, taping strips together and to the base as you go.

EASTER BUNNY CAKE

1 package cake mix	*4 red gum drops*
1 package fluffy white	*10-ounce package*
frosting	*shredded coconut*
Pink coloring	

Prepare cake mix according to package directions. Turn into Reynolds Wrap bunny pan. Spread batter into small areas and corners. Bake in preheated 350°F oven for 30 minutes. Cool on wire rack for 10 minutes. Pull foil edge from pan and cool cake. Leave on foil base and place on a tray. Frost with fluffy white frosting, reserving about 3 tablespoons frosting. Tint reserved frosting pink; spread on the ears and nose. Make eyes and whiskers with gum drops. Sprinkle with shredded coconut for fluffy effect.

Jelly rolls, the popular desserts of the Gay Nineties, and the more sophisticated cream rolls and chocolate rolls of the present day, are delightful, easy-to-prepare sweets. Whip up the batter with an electric mixer. Make the special pan for baking them from Heavy Duty Reynolds Wrap. Chill the rolled and filled cakes in the refrigerator or freeze them, tightly wrapped in foil.

Jelly Roll pan made of foil: Tear off a 24-inch piece of Heavy Duty Reynolds Wrap. Fold it in half to make a double-thick sheet 12 x 18 inches. Turn up edges 1 inch on all sides and miter corners for firmness. Grease lightly. Stand on cookie sheet for support.

BASIC SPONGE ROLL   *(10 servings)*

4 eggs	*¾ teaspoon baking*
1 teaspoon vanilla	* powder*
1 cup sugar	*¼ teaspoon salt*
1 cup sifted cake flour	

Beat eggs and vanilla at high speed of electric mixer or with rotary egg beater until thick and lemon colored. Gradually beat in sugar until mixture is fluffy and thick. Sift together the dry ingredients and add all at once, folding them in by hand. Pour into a 15 x 10 x 1 inch jelly roll pan that has been lined with foil, lightly greased, or into a lightly greased foil pan.

Bake the cake in a 375° oven 12 to 15 minutes, or until a very light brown. Do not overbake. Turn out on a large sheet of Reynolds Wrap which has been generously sprinkled with granulated sugar. Peel off foil lining or foil pan. Trim off crisp edges. Roll up and cover loosely with foil, leaving ends open. Let stand no more than 15 to 20 minutes. Unroll and spread with filling. Reroll, cover with foil, and chill about 1 hour in refrigerator before serving.

Jelly Filling: Whip any flavorful jelly; spread on cake. Apricot jam folded into whipped cream makes a splendid filling.

STRAWBERRY CREAM FILLING

1 pint strawberries	*½ pint heavy cream,*
½ cup sugar	* whipped*

Hull, rinse, and drain strawberries. Save a few of the best for garnish; slice the remainder, combine with sugar, and fold into the cream. Spread on the cool cake. Garnish with whole berries.

TIPS FOR COOKIE BAKERS

To bake cookies, tear off lengths of foil the same size as cookie pan. Place cookies on foil. As one sheetful is baked, slip foil off and put another cookie-dotted foil length on pan. Saves time.

It's not necessary to grease foil to prevent cookies from sticking unless cookies are made without shortening. Moisten pan with a few drops of water before placing foil on it to hold foil in position.

Remove cookies from foil while hot or warm. If they stick, put back in the oven for a few minutes.

Brownies and other bar-type cookies are easier to remove if the pan is lined with foil. To store: when cool, cover pan with foil, or remove foil with cookies and seal foil.

For fresh-baked cookies at a moment's notice, keep refrigerator cookie dough wrapped in foil in your refrigerator or freezer. Slice and bake as needed. Rewrap unused portion and return to refrigerator or freezer. Cookie dough keeps 2 weeks in the refrigerator, indefinitely in the freezer.

To store baked cookies, put them away in an envelope of foil. This can be placed in the bread and cake drawer of kitchen cabinet —cookies will stay crisp. Or freeze cookies: arrange on foil-covered cardboard in layers separated by foil and overwrap. Or pack in boxes and overwrap with foil. Frozen cookies should be placed on foil-covered cookie sheet in a 350°F oven 10 minutes to crisp.

Sending cookies through the mail: Brownies and other bar-type cookies and drop cookies are the easiest to mail. These may be wrapped individually or placed in a foil-lined box or can, in layers. Separate layers and cover top layer with foil. Reinforce container so it is strong enough to withstand handling in the mail.

ACCORDION TREATS *(4 dozen)*

¾ cup butter	*¼ teaspoon salt*
¾ cup sugar	*1¼ cups sifted*
2 eggs, unbeaten	*all-purpose flour*
1 teaspoon vanilla	

Preheat oven to 325°F. Cream butter; gradually add sugar, continuing to beat. Add eggs, vanilla, and salt; beat until light and fluffy. Gradually add flour, mixing in well. Fold 1 yard of foil lengthwise to double thickness, then fold into 1-inch accordion pleats. Place on cookie sheet or back of roasting pan. Drop dough by teaspoonfuls into folds. (Dough spreads in baking.) Bake 25 to 30 minutes, until a light golden brown. Cool 10 minutes. Remove cookies; reuse foil.

Quick way: Bake cookies made from a mix in accordion folds.

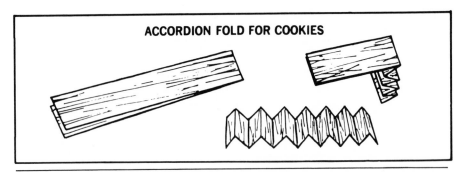

ACCORDION FOLD FOR COOKIES

PEANUT BUTTER REFRIGERATOR COOKIES   *(4 dozen)*

2 cups sifted all-purpose flour
1 teaspoon baking soda
½ teaspoon salt
1 cup soft butter or margarine
1 cup light brown sugar, firmly packed
1 cup chunk style peanut butter
1 egg
1 teaspoon vanilla

Sift together flour, soda, salt. Cream butter and sugar until light; beat in peanut butter, egg, vanilla. Mix in dry ingredients, blending thoroughly. Chill dough 30 minutes. Form into two long rolls, about 2 inches in diameter. Wrap in foil; chill 4 hours or freeze until needed. Preheat oven to 375°F. With very sharp knife slice rolls about ⅛ inch thick; place on a foil-covered cookie sheet. Bake 6 to 8 minutes, until lightly browned.

LEMON DROPS   *(3 dozen)*

½ cup butter
1 cup sugar
1 whole egg
2 yolks
1½ cups sifted flour
½ teaspoon baking powder
½ teaspoon salt
Grated rind of 1 large lemon
3 tablespoons lemon juice
½ cup coarsely chopped walnuts

Preheat oven to 350°F. Cream butter, sugar, whole egg and yolks together until light and fluffy. Sift the dry ingredients together and add alternately with the lemon rind and juice. Blend well. Stir in the nuts. Drop from teaspoon onto foil-lined cookie sheet 1½ inches apart. Bake 12 to 15 minutes. While cookies are hot, remove to cake rack.

Good to know: This is a medium-crisp, very lemony cookie.

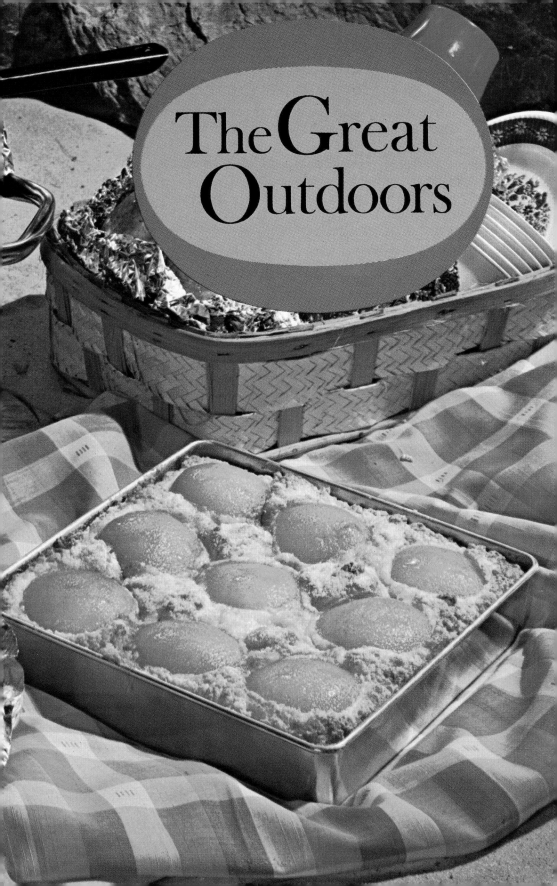

The Great Outdoors

The Great Outdoors

They cooked out-of-doors before foil was invented—
but what a difference it makes!

Cooking on a portable grill or outdoor fireplace is a fun way of preparing everyday meals and a great way of entertaining. You can turn out a delicious meal on a simple portable brazier-type grill or you can put on a chef's bonnet and barbecue with great flourish on de luxe electrically operated revolving spits or the new gas-fired outdoor grills.

The methods and recipes are all the same and all lead up to the well-known fact that everything tastes great cooked outdoors.

Building the fire: Some grills are simple bowl-shaped affairs without vents. Others may have vents in the bottom to permit air to enter, and some have a grate designed to hold the burning charcoal above the bottom surface. Whatever type you have, line the bottom surface with Heavy Duty Reynolds Wrap. Cut out openings to conform with vents.

The foil will hold the ashes and catch drippings. It reflects the heat upward to the food, thereby increasing the efficiency of the fire. Some outdoor chefs like to put a layer of coarse sand or fine stones over the foil to provide ventilation in grills not equipped with vents. This is not essential if you are burning charcoal.

Charcoal briquets give a long-lasting, steady-cooking fire. Shake them into the grill and ignite with a charcoal starter. There are several types of starters: the electric, which needs only to be plugged in and covered with charcoal; chemical solutions to pour or spray on; chimney-like devices which may be used to ignite quickly a small amount of charcoal and spread the fire to the rest of the coals.

To make a chimney fire starter: Cut out the ends of a large, tall cylindrical juice can (1-quart 14-ounce size) or a 2-pound coffee can. Use a beer-can opener to cut out V-shaped openings in one end. Punch out a few holes 1 inch above the end.

In color picture: Grilled Steak, Roasted Chicken, Golden Glory
Picnic Cake

Stand this in the center of a pile of charcoal. Fill the bottom with a crushed milk or cream carton or other kindling material, then fill the remainder of the can with charcoal. Light with a match at the bottom. The parafined cartons burn with great intensity and quickly ignite the charcoal in the can. As soon as the briquets have spots of grey, lift off the can, using tongs, and the fire will spread to all the charcoal in the pile.

It takes about 20 minutes for all the charcoal to ignite and be ready for cooking. The charcoal will have grey spots—it will not be red. Test the heat by holding your hand well above the fire. The briquets will burn for an hour or longer.

Wood fires: Every boy and girl scout knows how to build a wood fire. Heavy duty foil can be used under wood. Oak, hickory, and other nut and fruit tree woods make the most flavorful fires. Let wood burn to a bed of glowing coals.

How hot a fire to use: People usually make the mistake of building too hot a fire. It takes about 2 pounds of charcoal to cook a 5 to 6 pound steak, about 1½ inches thick. Steaks, chops and hamburgers need a moderately hot fire; chicken and frankfurters and most other foods, a relatively low fire. The amount of heat that reaches food may be regulated by moving the food nearer to or farther from the fire.

Broiling hints: Trim excess fat from meats before placing over fire. Be prepared to lift the meat away from the fire for a minute or two if flare-up occurs. Baking soda sprinkled on the fire helps to prevent flare-ups.

When cooking is finished: If a simple brazier-type grill is being used, gather the foil up over the briquets and smother the fire. On grills equipped with hoods, close the hood down tightly and close vents. This puts out the fire and usually this will save the briquets so that they will ignite and burn again when a new fire is built. When ready to dispose of ashes, pick up the foil and the grill will be left clean. Cover the grill between uses, to keep it clean and dry.

Foil to use for outdoor cooking: Heavy Duty Reynolds Wrap, either the 14-inch broiling foil or 18-inch all-purpose heavy duty foil is best for all outdoor cooking uses. It is possible to use standard 12-inch Reynolds Wrap for heating breads, potato chips and foods that require only warming. You can use two or more thicknesses of standard Reynolds Wrap for making pans, and other uses where great strength is not required.

DE LUXE HAMBURGERS

(8 servings)

2 pounds ground chuck or round	2 teaspoons Ac'cent
1½ teaspoons salt	8 hamburger buns, split
Freshly ground black pepper	Chili sauce
	Prepared mustard

Toss the meat lightly with the salt, pepper and Ac'cent. Form into 8 patties. Place patties on the grill over a medium hot fire and broil, turning once. About 4 minutes on a side is usually sufficient to grill hamburgers medium rare. Spread the buns with a little butter, and toast them around the outer, less hot, part of the grill during last few minutes while hamburgers are cooking. Place each hamburger on a toasted bun half and top with mustard, chili sauce and second half of bun. Serve piping hot with a selection of relishes, such as sliced dill pickles, slices of tomato and mild sweet onion.

Cheeseburgers: When you turn the hamburgers, place a slice of cheese on each, letting it melt while underside is broiling.

BROILED STEAK

A T-bone (porterhouse) or sirloin steak is the most tender and delicious steak for outdoor broiling. It should be at least 1½ inches thick. Remove it from the refrigerator about 1 hour before it is to be cooked. Trim excess fat and use a skewer if needed to make the steak compact. Have the fire moderately hot and place the steak on the grill 4 to 5 inches above the hot coals. Broil, turning once or twice, until a good brown on both sides. Have ready a warmed wooden plank or carving board; transfer the steak to the board. Spread quickly with softened butter or margarine, sprinkle with salt and pepper and chopped parsley. Carve steak in thin slices.

Broiled rump or round steak: Good quality rump or round has fine flavor, but is not as tender as porterhouse or sirloin. Select a steak that is 1½ to 2 inches thick. Sprinkle with meat tenderizer, following package directions. Or marinate the meat in the new instant marinade mix, according to package directions. If marinated, pat steak dry before broiling.

Handling heavy steaks: A long-handled, hinged-wire folding broiler can be used for holding steak while it broils. Grease the wire and place the steak between the two sides, securing it by tightening the little slip ring over the handle. This type of broiler makes it possible to lift and turn the steak easily. Have a large piece of foil handy by the grill so that when the steak is removed from the fire it may be rested on the foil. This will catch drippings.

HOW LONG TO BROIL

Steak Thickness	Time on each side, over a moderate fire		
	Rare	Medium	Well Done
1½ inches	7 minutes	9 minutes	10 minutes
2 inches	10 minutes	12 minutes	14 minutes
2½ inches	12 minutes	14 minutes	16 minutes

DOUBLE-THICK LAMB CHOPS
GRILLED WITH HERB BUTTER *(6 servings)*

6 loin lamb chops, cut
  double thick
½ cup butter or
  margarine
1 teaspoon chopped
  fresh tarragon
½ teaspoon chopped dill
½ teaspoon chopped
  rosemary
1 tablespoon chopped
  parsley
2 tablespoons dry red
  wine, vinegar, OR
  lemon juice
Salt and pepper

Remove excess fat from lamb chops and secure ends with toothpick. Place them over a medium fire and grill, turning several times until they are nicely brown. Centers should be pink; 2-inch chops will take about 7 minutes on each side. Combine the butter, herbs and wine in a small pan and heat and simmer for a few minutes at one side of grill. Sprinkle the chops well with salt and pepper and pour a spoonful or two of herb butter over each chop.

BUTTERFLY LEG OF LAMB VERMOUTH *(8 to 10 servings)*

1 6 to 7 pound leg of
  lamb
1 clove garlic (optional)
2 teaspoons salt
Generous grating black
  pepper
1 teaspoon fresh OR
½ teaspoon dried
  rosemary
1 cup dry vermouth
2 tablespoons olive or
  salad oil

Have the lamb boned at the market or do it yourself. Remove excess fat and sinews. If you like garlic, cut clove in half and rub meat on both sides. Sprinkle with the seasonings, particularly on the cut side. Place the meat in a hinged wire broiler, spreading it out as you would a steak. Grill the lamb over a rather low fire, turning it several times. Heat the vermouth and oil in a small saucepan and brush over the meat several times during the broiling. It should take about 30 minutes to grill the lamb to a beautiful brown color and have the inside still juicy and pink. Place the meat on a warm carving board and spread with a little softened butter or margarine and chopped parsley. Slice in thin slices. Simmer remaining vermouth for a few minutes, then pour over each serving.

BARBECUED CHICKEN

Shopping: If you are serving a half chicken to each person, buy 1½-pound broiler-fryers. If chicken is to be quartered, buy 2- to 2½-pound chickens. If chicken is to be cut in serving-size pieces buy 2- to 3-pound chickens. Figure a little more than ½ pound of chicken for each person.

Preparation: Rinse chicken and pat dry. Remove fat and any bones that pull out easily. Brush the chicken lightly with salad oil, melted butter or margarine, and season with salt and pepper. Have a low fire burning in the grill. Place chicken on the grill and broil slowly, turning frequently for 35 to 45 minutes. Baste with barbecue sauce after the chicken is almost as brown as desired.

Serving: Have ready inexpensive small baskets or paper plates. Place squares of foil on each. As chicken finishes cooking, place servings on the foil; bring corners of foil together over chicken and twist to make a loose poke. This keeps chicken hot.

LEMON-HERB BARBECUE SAUCE

½ cup salad oil
¼ cup lemon juice
½ cup water
1 teaspoon salt
3 tablespoons brown sugar

1 teaspoon dry mustard
½ teaspoon each: dried thyme, rosemary, tarragon

Combine ingredients and heat to boiling point. Keep hot while basting chicken. Makes 1¼ cups, enough to baste 3 chickens.

TEXAS BARBECUE SAUCE

1 cup catsup
¼ cup cider vinegar
1 teaspoon chili powder
⅓ cup Worcestershire

3 drops Tabasco sauce
2 teaspoons salt
¾ cup water
¼ cup salad oil

Combine all ingredients, bring to boil. Keep hot while basting. Makes 2½ cups, enough to baste 4 or 5 chickens.

FISH ON THE GRILL

Most fish have a tendency to fall apart when placed on the grate of a grill and they are difficult to turn. A good-size, firm-fleshed fish, such as a rockfish, striped bass, bluefish or salmon, may be split and placed in the folding wire broiler for grilling. Several small fish may also be handled this way.

Other fish are best wrapped in foil, with seasonings, and cooked on the grate over the coals. Both methods are fine—the first yields a browned crisp-skinned fish and the second a moist, flavorful fish with delicious juices.

Removing fish from a wire broiler: Fish tends to stick, so be sure the wires or rods of the broiler are well greased before placing fish in it. When done, place the broiler over a large piece of Reynolds Wrap. Carefully loosen the fish from the wires of top half of broiler. Now fold back this section of the broiler and turn, resting fish on serving platter. Again, loosen the fish away from wires on second side of broiler, and it will be free and resting on platter.

GRILLED STRIPED BASS   *(6 to 8 servings)*

1 3-pound striped bass   **1 teaspoon salt**
½ cup butter or   **Generous grating black**
  margarine   **pepper**
¼ cup lemon juice
½ teaspoon each fresh
  OR ¼ teaspoon dried:
  thyme, rosemary

Remove head and tail from fish and split it for broiling. Grease a folding wire broiler and place the fish in it. Brush with the butter and lemon juice. Sprinkle with all the seasonings. Broil over medium hot fire, turning frequently and brushing with the butter and lemon mixture several times. Broil 12 to 15 minutes or until fish can be flaked with a fork.

Good to know: Grill salmon and bluefish in the same manner. Serve with lemon wedges.

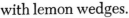

GRILLED MONTAUK POINT SWORDFISH STEAK
(10 servings)

*1 6-pound swordfish
    steak, 1 to 1½ inches
    thick
3 tablespoons melted
    butter or salad oil
Salt and coarsely ground
    black pepper*

*½ cup butter or
    margarine
½ teaspoon each:
    tarragon, rosemary,
    thyme
1 cup dry white wine
Chopped parsley*

Wipe the fish steak and place it on one section of a folding wire broiler. Brush with melted butter or salad oil, season well with salt and pepper. Close broiler, turn over, open and give second side of fish the same treatment. Fasten two sides of broiler together and place the fish over a *hot* fire. Broil as quickly as possible. Swordfish has little fat and is somewhat difficult to brown. Fifteen to 20 minutes total broiling time should be sufficient. Heat the butter, herbs, and wine at one side of grill and, during last few minutes the fish is broiling, brush with a little of this sauce. When the fish is done, transfer to a hot platter or plank (note directions, page 171). Simmer the wine sauce a few minutes longer and pour over the fish. Sprinkle with chopped parsley.

This is an easy method of cooking fish over the coals, one preferred by many avid fishermen. Former President Eisenhower grilled trout by this method. As with any food cooked over the coals in a foil package, the foil is sealed as tightly as possible. In turning, some juice is bound to seep out—but no one minds, since you are cooking out of doors. The fish will be moist and sweet.

WHOLE FISH GRILLED IN FOIL
*Butter or margarine
1 medium onion, sliced
    thin
1 to 3 pound fish,
    cleaned, head and tail
    removed*

*Salt and pepper
Fresh tarragon, parsley,
    dill, thyme, rosemary
Butter*

Tear off a suitable-size piece of heavy duty foil. Spread a little butter or margarine in the center and put some of the onion slices on it. Place the fish on the onion slices. Sprinkle fish cavity with salt and pepper. Arrange remaining onion slices and herbs over fish. Sprinkle with salt and pepper and dot generously with butter. Bring foil up over fish, sealing edges with double fold. Seal both ends with double fold. Place on grate over medium hot fire. Cook a 1-pound fish about 15 minutes, 2-pound fish 25 minutes, 3-pound fish 35 minutes, turning two or three times. To serve, transfer foil with fish to a serving dish—a shingle will do if you are camping—open foil, turn back and crimp edges. Fish may be lifted right off the bones. Spoon juices in foil over each serving.

SCAMPI *(12 servings)*

2 pounds shrimp, fresh or frozen,with shell	*3 tablespoons lemon juice* **OR**
1 small clove garlic, finely minced	*1½ tablespoons lemon juice plus 1½ tablespoons dry*
1 cup butter or margarine, melted	*white wine*
¼ teaspoon each: rosemary, basil	*½ teaspoon salt*
	¼ teaspoon freshly ground pepper

If shrimp are frozen with shell, thaw just to separate. Rinse in cold water, drain and place in boiling water. Bring to a boil and cook 1 minute. Drain; cool just enough to handle. Remove shells and dark vein. If frozen shrimp are already shelled and cleaned, use only 1 pound and thaw until they can be separated.

Mince garlic; add to butter with herbs. Let stand over heat for a few minutes to frizzle the garlic. Add lemon juice. Arrange 5 or 6 shrimp to a serving on squares of heavy duty foil. Pour butter mixture over; sprinkle each serving with salt and pepper. Bring foil up over shrimp, and twist ends together at top to seal. Place on grill over medium hot fire and grill for 10 to 12 minutes. Serve bundles on paper plates—each person opens his own.

You don't need to wait until you are at the shore to enjoy a clambake. Most supermarkets today carry lobsters and clams, and a portable grill can be used to cook a superb clambake. This famous combination of seafood, chicken, and vegetables can be cooked in heavy duty foil, enough for 1 person in each package.

BACKYARD CLAMBAKE   *(1 serving)*

12 steamer clams	*1 small onion, quartered*
1 1-pound lobster	*Salt and pepper*
½ small broiler-fryer	*Melted butter*
1 ear of corn	
1 potato, cut lengthwise in eighths	

You will also need a 1-yard square of cheesecloth for each serving. If lobster comes with seaweed, or if you live where you can get it, have a handful of seaweed for each serving.

Scrub the clams, rinse and split the lobster, and remove as many sharp bones from chicken as come out easily. Shuck the corn. Tear off large squares of heavy duty foil and have ready squares of cheesecloth somewhat larger. Place cheesecloth on top of the foil. If you have seaweed, put a handful on the cheesecloth; top with chicken, then the lobster and clams. Tuck in the corn, onion, potato wherever there is room. Shake on freshly ground pepper, salt. If you haven't used seaweed, add 4 tablespoons water to each package. Tie the cheesecloth up over the food, then seal the foil to make an airtight package.

Place the packages on the grill over a medium hot fire and cook about 45 minutes to 1 hour. Open a package at end of 35 minutes to test the chicken for doneness. Reclose and continue cooking, if not done. Prepare melted butter and pour into individual dishes for each person. Serve packages on paper plates.

Great go-with: Lots of good cold beer for this feast!

GRILL ROASTING AND SMOKE COOKING

This is a wonderful way of cooking turkey, roasts of beef, lamb, and all meats "over the coals." It adds a delightful tinge of charcoal flavor to these foods, makes them very crisp on the outside and somewhat more ruddy in color. It does not char foods or overbrown them if done properly—and it's a very easy method of cooking.

You will need a grill with a hood or dome-type cover that can be completely closed over the food. Vents or dampers in the bottom of the grill and in the hood can be used to regulate the fire so that your grill becomes an oven.

Grills with hoods are available in department and hardware stores.

You can make a hood from wire coat hangers and Heavy Duty Reynolds Wrap to fit a sizable brazier-type grill. This will work very well and, if stored out of harm's way between uses, will last a long time. Directions for making foil hood are on page 176.

Here are a few simple steps to follow for smoke roasting:

1. Line the grill with heavy duty foil as usual.

2. Build the fire *at one side* of the grill, rather than in the center. About half a 5-pound bag of charcoal makes a long-lasting fire that will cook a turkey.

3. Place an inexpensive foil-lined shallow pan on the other side of the grill bottom to catch drippings.

4. Place grill rack to hold food in position. Usually there is a little section which opens for adding briquets. Have this over the fire.

5. Light the fire. When the briquets are burning well, close the hood over the grill and adjust vents so fire burns as you wish.

6. Open and place turkey or roast on the rack over pan; close hood over the food. You will have to judge the temperature inside by how quickly the food browns. Open vents more if too slow; close if too fast.

A meat thermometer may be used to check doneness of food, just as in the oven. Should the side toward the fire tend to brown a little too fast, protect it with a small piece of foil. Basting is not essential, but helps to add even more delicious flavor.

If the fire burns slowly it usually lasts throughout a 2 to 3 hour roasting. Additional briquets can be added if needed.

Because the drippings do not fall into the fire, there is no great amount of smoke formed—in fact very little, but enough to give meats delectable new flavor. If you want a more pronounced smoke flavor, add damp hickory chips or sawdust, or twigs cut from a wild cherry or other backyard fruit tree. Add them toward the end of the roasting time and the flavor will not be too heavy.

It takes just about the same length of time to roast by the smoke cooking grill method as in the oven of the kitchen range. And you can roast on the grill the year round—but be sure to place your grill out of the wind in cold weather.

Remember this cooking method on a busy holiday—it will free the oven for pies and desserts!

COAT-HANGER HOOD FOR GRILL

1. With wire cutters, clip hooks off 6 or 7 coat hangers; straighten wire with pliers.

2. Form 2 or more lengths into a firm circle, using picture wire to bind ends together. This is the base of hood, and should fit just inside grill.

3. Loop remaining wires umbrella-fashion and attach to base circle, using pliers to twist ends. Fasten together at top with picture wire.

4. Cover with Heavy Duty Reynolds Wrap. Leave small portion of foil loose at top to open for draft.

FOIL HOOD FOR GRILL

SMOKED TURKEY

To deeply smoke a turkey for party or buffet serving, prepare the turkey for roasting in the usual way, but do not stuff. Instead, put ½ cup coarsely chopped mixed celery and parsley in neck and body cavities. Have the fire in the grill burning very slowly and add damp hickory chips several times during the roasting. Allow six or seven hours to smoke a 12 to 14 pound bird. Baste with cider or wine, if desired. Tests for doneness are the same as for grill-roasted turkey. The meat thermometer should read 185°F. Drippings serve as sauce. Turkey can be served warm or cold.

FOLLOW DIRECTIONS (page 175) AND GRILL ROAST THESE MEATS:

Turkey: Prepare the turkey for roasting in the usual way (page 56). Stuff if desired. Have grill fire moderate. Baste with a mixture of: ½ cup melted butter or margarine, 1 cup dry wine and ½ teaspoon mixed herbs. A 15-pound turkey takes about 4½ hours. The meat thermometer should read 185°F.

Beef: A rolled roast or boneless sirloin is easiest to manage. If standing rib is used, have bone end cut short. Have the grill fire moderately hot. Baste the roast occasionally with 1 cup dry red wine. A 6-pound boneless rolled roast, 4 inches thick, should take about 2½ hours to roast medium done. The meat thermometer should read 160°F.

Leg of Lamb: Rub roast with a small clove of garlic crushed into 2 teaspoons salt and coarsely ground black pepper, or with salt, mixed herbs and grated lemon rind. Have fire moderate. Baste with 1 cup rosé wine. A 7 to 8 pound leg of lamb will take about 2½ hours. The meat thermometer should read 175°F.

Ham: Remove skin on a fully cooked ham and trim excess fat. Score remaining fat. Have the fire rather low, add hickory chips or twigs or fruit wood during last hour. Baste with 1 cup cider or sherry. If you want a glaze on the ham, about 20 minutes before it is done brush with a thin paste made by combining ½ cup cider or sherry with ½ cup brown sugar and 1 tablespoon prepared mustard. A 15-pound, fully cooked ready-to-eat ham takes about 2½ hours. The meat thermometer should read 130°F.

SPIT ROASTING

In selecting meats or poultry to be roasted or barbecued over a charcoal fire on a revolving spit, choose those that are as regular in shape as possible. Boned and tied roasts of beef, lamb, or pork are good. Chickens and small turkeys should be securely trussed, ducks should have their legs and wings tied together. Insert spit through the meat in such a way that the weight will be evenly distributed, so that spit will revolve smoothly. Insert prongs at either end of meat and fasten securely.

If you are not experienced, it is well to spit the meat, place it in position and rotate it while the grill is cold, to be sure it is evenly and correctly balanced.

Build the fire at the back of the grill. Form a pan of heavy duty foil and place it at the front of the fire, adjusting so that juices will drop onto it. This permits basting with a sauce and saving juices to be served with the meat—and prevents juice from dropping into the fire.

SPIT-ROASTED DUCKLING
WITH ORANGE BARBECUE SAUCE   *(4 servings)*

*1 5-pound eviscerated
    duckling*
1 stalk celery with leaves
2 or 3 sprigs parsley

1 small onion, quartered
*½ small orange with
    skin, cut up*
Salt and pepper

Remove pin feathers, excess skin and fat of duck, and rinse. Salt and pepper cavity and place in it the celery, parsley, onion, orange. Truss securely with skewers and string. Spit the duck and place in position over a moderate fire. Place foil pan at front of fire to catch drippings. Set spit in motion and roast the duck slowly. Baste every 15 minutes with Orange Barbecue Sauce, using a bulb baster or brush. Roast about 2 hours for a 5-pound duck.

When duck is done, remove to a hot platter. Remove foil drip pan and pour drippings into saucepan. Skim off fat and add remaining barbecue sauce. Simmer the juices on grill until sauce is slightly thickened. Add salt and pepper to taste. Garnish duck with orange sections.

ORANGE BARBECUE SAUCE

Grated rind of 1 orange
¾ cup orange juice
*2 tablespoons lemon
    juice*
⅓ cup light brown sugar

½ teaspoon salt
*Generous grating black
    pepper*
*A pinch each: rosemary,
    thyme*

Combine all ingredients in small saucepan; heat to melt sugar.

VEGETABLES OVER THE COALS

Foil-roasted corn and potatoes are favorites. Everybody loves them. And there are different and fine ways of cooking these standbys—many ways of cooking other vegetables too. A foil package can be your saucepan on the grill, and you can serve in it, as well! *Potatoes Roasted over the Coals:* Scrub potatoes, dry, rub with a little butter, margarine, or bacon fat. Wrap in foil. Place on grill over moderate fire and roast 50 minutes for medium-size potato. Or place around outer edge of grill and allow slightly longer. If space is tight, place potatoes around outer edge of fire, right on the coals. Turn two or three times. Pierce through foil with fork to test doneness or squeeze with fingers protected by gloves. To serve, slit foil, squeeze slightly to fluff up centers, top with butter.

Great go-with: Pass sour cream and chives, cottage cheese, crumbled bacon to go with roasted potatoes.

Patio Potatoes: Prepare potatoes as for French fries, or use frozen French fries. Place enough to serve the crowd in center of large square of heavy duty foil. Add minced onion, salt and pepper, snips of fresh dill or a sprinkling of the dried, and dot with butter. Use less butter for frozen French fries. Close package loosely and place over a medium fire. Cook 40 minutes for fresh, about 25 minutes for frozen potatoes. To serve, turn back foil and place package in a basket. Potatoes will brown slightly through the foil.

Foil-Roasted Corn: Husks may be left on or removed. If left on, pull back and remove silk, brush with melted butter or margarine, sprinkle with seasonings. Replace husks, wrap in foil, twisting ends to secure. If husks are removed, spread corn with softened butter or margarine and season. Wrap in foil, double-wrapping if fire is very hot or if corn is to be placed on the coals. Roast for about 25 minutes, turning two or three times.

Whole Onions: Select medium to large white or yellow onions. Rinse, leave skins on; place each on a square of heavy duty aluminum foil. Bring foil up over onions and twist together at top. Place on grill over medium fire and cook 40 to 50 minutes, turning occasionally. Onions are done when soft to the touch. Open foil. Skin will push back easily. Add butter, salt and pepper.

Zucchini, Tomatoes, and Onions: Slice zucchini, cut peeled tomatoes in quarters, slice onions very thin. Combine enough for the number to be served on a large square of heavy duty foil. Season with salt, pepper, a few snips of garlic, and basil. Dot with butter. Bring foil over vegetables and seal to make a tight package. Place on grill over medium fire and cook about 30 minutes, turning once. Serve right from package. This is also delicious made with summer squash.

Dilled Summer Squash: Slice tender young summer squash in ½-inch slices and slice an onion very thin. Arrange in the center of a square of heavy duty foil. Season with salt, pepper and snips of fresh dill or a generous sprinkling of the dried. Dot with butter. Seal package and cook over moderate heat, shaking occasionally, about 25 minutes.